*This book is a gift to:*

D.D.W.O. Anja Schwartz

*From:*

Cape Western Home League Ladies

*Date:*

Home League Rally September 2005

*Message:*

May God bless you and always
Keep you close to Him.

# A HEARTBEAT of Hope

366 DEVOTIONS

May the God of hope fill you with all joy
and peace as you trust in Him.
*Romans 15:13*

Nina Smit

CHRISTIAN ART PUBLISHERS

Published in South Africa by Christian Art Publishers
PO Box 1599, Vereeniging, 1930


First edition 2004

Adapted from *In Touch with God*

Translated by Lynette Douglas

Cover designed by Christian Art Publishers



Set in 13 on 15 pt Palatino by Christian Art Publishers

Printed in China

ISBN 1-86920-439-5



04 05 06 07 08 09 10 11 12 13 – 10 9 8 7 6 5 4 3 2

*For Renche*

♡

# JANUARY

# A brand new year

*"The Lord himself goes before you and will be with you; he will never leave you nor forsake you. Do not be afraid; do not be discouraged."*

~ DEUTERONOMY 31:8 ~

Today is the first day of a brand new year! A year in which you have nothing to fear, because God knows the path that lies before you. You have His promise that He will go before you, that each day of this new year He will be with you. You have His assurance that He will never leave you nor forsake you.

That is why you can confidently face the challenges and crises that may lie ahead of you this year.

*Today is the first day of the rest of your life.*

~ TRADITIONAL SAYING ~

What will you do this year to ensure that each day is a day of success and victory?

# The right road

*Let the morning bring me word of your unfailing love, for I have put my trust in you. Show me the way I should go, for to you I lift up my soul.*

~ PSALM 143:8 ~

The psalmist prays that God will cause him to walk on a straight path through life. He puts his hope in God because He knows that God has prepared a future in heaven for all His children.

At the beginning of a new year we all hope that our year will be pleasant and problem-free. This year, place your hope in God alone and you will become aware of His wonders around you in a new way every day. Stay close to Him, and He will direct you along the right paths.

*Don't squander time, it is the stuff that life is made of.*

~ BENJAMIN FRANKLIN ~

What will you do this year to overcome problems on your path through life?

# God knows

*Does he not see my ways and count my every step?*

~ JOB 31:4 ~

The year ahead is unknown territory. Not one of us can know what challenges we might have to face. But God already knows what you will go through this year. He is completely in control of your future. He can defuse every crisis. And if you love and serve Him, He promises to be by your side each day, to keep an eye on you at all times, to watch over every step that you take.

*Worry is the natural result of placing our hope in anything other than in God's will for our lives.*

~ BILLY GRAHAM ~

What problems in your life give you the most concern?

# Make the most of each day

*This is the day the LORD has made; let us rejoice and be glad in it.*
~ PSALM 118:24 ~

Each new day is a gift straight from the hand of God – a gift guaranteed to give you joy and make you happy.

There are still 361 such gifts for you to use and enjoy this year. Make the most of each day of the new year – each day comes only once, and once it has past, you can never get it back again. Use every opportunity that comes your way, and rejoice in each one!

*We do not know how long we will live, and for that very reason, we have an obligation to live each day to the fullest.*
~ HENRI NOUWEN ~

How will you make sure that you use every opportunity that comes your way this year?

To witness - share with others what God has done in my life - what He can do in & through their lives.

# An angel will watch over you

*See, I am sending an angel ahead of you to guard you along the way and to bring you to the place I have prepared.*

~ EXODUS 23:20 ~

God has promised that He will send an angel to protect you on the unknown road into the future – an angel who will make sure that you ultimately reach the destination that God Himself has prepared for you.

Make sure that you are sensitive to what the angel of God says to you and that you obey his instructions in every aspect. If you do this, you will be assured of God's protection every day.

*When you enter the realm of God's love, you find written on the door: Fear Forbidden.*

~ KARL BARTH ~

What do you fear in the days and months ahead?

Lectures (me doing some!)

Timetable @ College

# God will lead you

*If you spend yourselves in behalf of the hungry and satisfy the needs of the oppressed, then your light will rise in the darkness, and your night will become like the noonday.*

~ ISAIAH 58:10 ~

God will be your guide through the year that lies ahead, as long as you are, in turn, prepared to reach out a helping hand to your fellowman. What you do for other people, you do indirectly for the Lord. Make a decision right now that you will be sensitive to the needs of others. Ask the Lord to open your eyes and ears to the needs of others, and do not put off doing something practical to help them. Then you will live in His light this year.

*The only justification for our existence is that we do good to others.*

~ GERHARD BEUKES ~

How will you help others this year?

# The Lord will be your help

*If the LORD delights in a man's way, he makes his steps firm.*

~ PSALM 37:23 ~

The Lord wants to guide you through this new year. He wants to support and help you in everything that you undertake this year. He wants to reveal to you how He wants you to live. He wants to direct your path.

The promise in this verse comes with a condition: God will support and guide you as long as you live according to His ways. Live each day in such a way that God will be pleased with the things you do and say.

*Those who love have big arms.*

~ CLAERHOUT ~

In what areas do you most have need of God's help?

# Put your hope in God

*O LORD, be gracious to us; we long for you. Be our strength every morning, our salvation in time of distress.*

~ ISAIAH 33:2 ~

The people of God turned to Him for help time and time again when things went terribly wrong for them. And He was always willing to respond to their cries.

In the unknown year that lies before you, you can confidently place your hope in God each day: He is still a refuge for His children in times of trouble. He will help you and strengthen you, as He has always done for His children.

*Today well-lived makes every tomorrow a vision of Hope.*
~ AUTHOR UNKNOWN ~

What are your hopes for this year?

# God is always near

*Your name, O LORD, endures forever, your renown, O LORD, through all generations.*

~ PSALM 135:13 ~

The children of God cannot live without Him. God is eternal and unchanging. He proves His support and trustworthy love from one generation to another to those who love Him and serve Him. Even though we may sometimes be unfaithful to Him, He remains faithful to us.

There is one fact that you can carry with you through this year: God is with you. He will never forsake you. When you have need of Him, you can call on Him – He will never disappoint you.

*When you need to make your own way through life, there is no greater support than that which is found in the presence of God.*

~ JOHAN SMIT ~

In what areas do you need God's support?

# The right road

*Although the LORD gives you the bread of adversity and the water of affliction ... Whether you turn to the right or to the left, your ears will hear a voice behind you, saying, "This is the way; walk in it."*

~ ISAIAH 30:20-21 ~

Parents discipline their children when they are disobedient. In the same way, God sometimes allows troubling times to come to those of His children who stray from the right road. In this way He brings them back to Him.

If you wander away from God, He might allow you to go through difficulties so that you will learn to know His will. Through suffering, He will bring you back on the right road. Remember that crises in your life are often God's way of drawing you closer to Him – and take the opportunity to learn from them.

*Everything that causes me to suffer,*
*also makes a better man of me.*

~ BENJAMIN FRANKLIN ~

What have you learned from the crises in your life?

# The Love of Jesus

*So that you may be able to discern what is best and may be pure and blameless until the day of Christ, filled with the fruit of righteousness that comes through Jesus Christ – to the glory and praise of God.*

~ PHILIPPIANS 1:10-11 ~

If you believe in Jesus, He will help you to live righteously. The love of Jesus will change your life forever because it changes your priorities and brings you into a right relationship with God.

Therefore, the closer you live to Jesus, the more others will see how wonderful God is through all that you do. Make your resolution this year to be led by the love of Jesus and to become more and more like Him.

*God's love is free, but it is not cheap. Let us honor it.*

~ A. S. ~

What adjustments do you need to make to your priorities?

# Love means …

*And this is my prayer: that your love may abound more and more in knowledge and depth of insight, so that you may be able to discern what is best and may be pure and blameless until the day of Christ.*

~ PHILIPPIANS 1:9-10 ~

If Jesus' love is in your life, you will be able to understand other people better. The love of Jesus compels you to care for your fellowman and it creates in you a sensitivity for the needs of others.

Live close to Jesus. Ask Him to cause His love to grow in you day by day this year so that your understanding and compassion will increase and you will make the right decisions and choices.

*Love heals people – those who*
*receive it as well as those who give it.*
~ KARL MENNINGER ~

In what areas of your life will
you give more love this year?

# Love and prayers

*"But I tell you: Love your enemies and pray for those who persecute you."*

~ MATTHEW 5:44 ~

It is easy to pray for the people you love. But it is a completely different thing to pray for those who stand in your way, who outshine you in various areas, those who do their best to belittle you. And yet Jesus expects this of you.

The people who least deserve your love and prayers usually need it the most. Set aside a special time each day this year to pray for them.

*When we fold our hands in prayer, God opens His hands.*

~ GERMAN PROVERB ~

Write down the prayer requests that you have for this year.

# Never alone

*Praise be to the LORD, to God our Savior, who daily bears our burdens.*
~ PSALM 68:19 ~

A Christian is someone who is never alone – God is with him every day. And because God is with him, he has the assurance that God will help and support him. He knows that God will carry him when he feels he cannot take another step.

God promises to carry you this year too. He undertakes to give you enough strength for each day. If things become too hard for you this year, you can lean on God's strength moment by moment.

*To have faith in God is to begin again*
*each morning as if it were completely new.*
~ C. S. LEWIS ~

What do you need God's strength for today?

# The love of Jesus envelopes you

*I pray that you may grasp how wide and long and high and deep is the love of Christ, and to know this love that surpasses knowledge.*

~ Ephesians 3:18-19 ~

Jesus' love for you is so all-embracing that it fills every area of your life to overflowing. We cannot find the words to describe His love. We cannot understand how a holy God can have so much love for unworthy sinners. But we can accept this love for ourselves.

The closer you live to God this year, the more the love He demonstrated in Jesus Christ will become a reality in your life.

*The essence of Christian love is not the desire to love but the certainty that God loves you.*

~ Thomas Merton ~

Write your own definition of the love of Christ in the space below.

An unconditional love without limits!

# God is faithful to His promises

*Let us hold unswervingly to the hope we profess, for he who promised is faithful.*

~ HEBREWS 10:23 ~

For those people who continue to hope in God, things go well, because God is absolutely faithful to each one of His promises. They do not lose their hope, even in times of hardship.

Even when it seems at times that one of these promises is not being fulfilled in your life, you should still hold fast to the promises of God. Keep hoping in God. He is faithful. He will fulfill each one of His promises for your life at exactly the right time. Trust Him for that!

*There are no hopeless situations in life.*
*There are only people who have given up hope.*
~ CLAIRE BOOTH LURA ~

Write down your favorite Bible promise.

Be still and know that I am God!
Ps. 46:10

# God offers peace

*My heart is not proud, O LORD, my eyes are not haughty; I do not concern myself with great matters or things too wonderful for me. But I have stilled and quieted my soul; like a weaned child with its mother, like a weaned child is my soul within me.*

~ PSALM 131:1-2 ~

There is no more beautiful picture of absolute contentment than that of a baby asleep in its mother's arms. God wants to give you the same kind of complete contentment this year. God offers you His peace in exchange for your anxiety. If you are willing to wait for Him, He will cause His rest and peace to permeate your life. You can leave your worries and concerns with Him. Will you accept this offer of His?

*The rainbow of God's promises spans the storms in our lives.*
~ CHARLES SHEPSON ~

Write a list of all the things that cause you stress, and then give the list to God.

My children - their spiritual well-being

# Absolute surrender

*May God himself, the God of peace, sanctify you through and through. May your whole spirit, soul and body be kept blameless at the coming of our Lord Jesus Christ.*

~ 1 THESSALONIANS 5:23 ~

The secret of inner peace is absolute surrender to God. Surrender means that you willingly give your whole life to God. To do only what He wants you to do. To put Him first in all things. To submit your will to His in all things.

If you successfully yield everything to Him, you will live each day in the shelter of His love this year.

*Peace becomes real when I consciously adjust the course of my life day by day to align with what I know about the will of God.*

~ MARETHA MAARTENS ~

In what areas of your life have you not given the reins to the Holy Spirit?

# You can be courageous

*"I have told you these things, so that in me you may have peace. In this world you will have trouble. But take heart! I have overcome the world."*

~ JOHN 16:33 ~

None of us can escape problems and crises. Sometimes it feels as if all the negative things we face in life knock us off course. If you are feeling desperate today, Jesus' message is meant especially for you: although you can expect to encounter difficulties, it is still possible to keep your head above water because Jesus has overcome the world. With His power at your disposal, you too will be an overcomer this year!

*Discouraged? Only until we hear the Almighty draw near.*

~ WILLIAM GURNALL ~

Write down the things that make you feel discouraged.

# Dependent on God

*We were under great pressure, far beyond our ability to endure, so that we despaired even of life ... But this happened that we might not rely on ourselves but on God, who raises the dead.*

~ 2 CORINTHIANS 1:8-9 ~

When everything in life is going well, we sometimes imagine that we can get by without God. If our bank account is flush, we don't see the need for praying for our daily bread ...

But life has a way of knocking us off our feet. That is when we realize that difficult times are actually beneficial because they teach us exactly how much we do need to depend on God. Remember this next time a crisis erupts in your life.

*Peace is not the absence of conflict*
*from life, but the ability to cope with it.*
~ UNKNOWN ~

Where do you need God's help most today?

# Look through His eyes

*For we are God's workmanship, created in Christ Jesus to do good works, which God prepared in advance for us to do.*

~ EPHESIANS 2:10 ~

You are the work of God's hands. And you are exceedingly wonderfully made. He created you for good works – and you will only truly understand His purpose for your life when you look at the world through His eyes.

Make an effort to make a positive difference in the lives of the people and the world around you this year. Live in such a way that the world will be a better place because you were prepared to make God's dream come true.

*Lord, strengthen me to do Thy will;*
*then mayest Thou ask me what Thou will.*
~ AUGUSTINE ~

What will you do this year to make a positive difference in the world around you?

# Live your faith

*As the body without the spirit is dead, so faith without deeds is dead.*
~ JAMES 2:26 ~

It is essential for Christians to be obedient to God, to do the things that He asks of them. It doesn't help to tell people that we believe in Christ if our lifestyle contradicts our words. If that is so, then James declares that we are actually dead.

If you believe in Christ, your faith should be evident in everything you say, do and think, otherwise you will be nothing more than a walking, breathing corpse! Make a decision right now to live like a child of God this year.

*Faith in God enables us to handle the mysteries of life.*
~ DANIËL LOUW ~

In what ways will you live as a child of God this year?

# True faith

*Do not say to your neighbor, "Come back later; I'll give it tomorrow" – when you now have it with you.*

~ PROVERBS 3:28 ~

True faith requires that you take note of the needs of the people around you and do something tangible to help them. If you do not help and love the people whom you can see, it is not possible for you to love God whom you cannot see, John writes in 1 John 4:20.

Let your love for God be evident in your actions. This year, show how much you love God by reaching out to other people, and helping them – without delay!

*Love is the means through which the theory of faith is worked out in practical deeds.*
~ JOHAN SMIT ~

What two things can you do today that will help others?

# We all like to ask

*Jesus asked, "Were not all ten cleansed? Where are the other nine?"*

~ LUKE 17:17 ~

Of the ten lepers whom Jesus healed, only one came back to thank Him. Many people live lives of ingratitude. We are all eager to ask God for things and then when we receive them, we so easily forget to thank Him. Make living with gratitude in your heart one of your resolutions this year. Stop taking the blessings of God for granted. Make an effort to thank God each day for one thing for which you have never thanked Him before.

*Gratitude is spiritual health made audible.*

~ C. S. LEWIS ~

Write down two things for which you have never before thanked God.

# Peace in your life

*Let the peace of Christ rule in your hearts, since as members of one body you were called to peace. And be thankful.*

~ COLOSSIANS 3:15 ~

We all want peace in our lives. But in the world around us, and even in our own lives, we see very little of God's peace. Instead of the peace that Christ gives, we are surrounded by violence and unrest.

Yet it is possible to live in peace with God and with others. If you allow God to be the referee over the conflicts in your life this year, and if you accept His decisions, you will experience His peace in your life.

*Biblical peace is not turning away from others, but embracing them.*

~ JOHAN SMIT ~

With what things (and people) have you not made peace in your life?

# Anchor your faith in Jesus Christ

*Such is the destiny of all who forget God; so perishes the hope of the godless. What he trusts in is fragile; what he relies on is a spider's web.*

~ JOB 8:13-14 ~

Job was bitter because things were going so badly for him and yet so well for the unbelievers around him. He could not understand God's way of doing things. But when he considered the final outcome of wickedness, a glimmer of understanding broke through. They have no hope for tomorrow. While unbelievers build their lives on a spider's web of hope, believers are anchored in the Rock of Jesus Christ. If you ever begin to doubt God's goodness toward you, hold fast to the "hope of glory" that God has promised to His children.

*Faith is a living relationship of trust in the Lord, in which you depend on Him completely.*

~ FERDINAND DEIST ~

Can you think of a verse that will be like a lifebelt when you founder in the sea of doubt?

# The initiative of love

*We love because he first loved us.*

~ 1 JOHN 4:19 ~

God's love for us is a gift of grace. And our love for God is also a gift of His grace. Grace means that the initiative of love always originates with God. It is only because God first loved us, while we were yet sinners, that the death of Christ on the cross made it possible for us to become His children. And for us to be able to love Him in return. We are not able to love in our own strength – not God and not our fellowmen. It is God who initiates love in the hearts of His children.

*We will not find the definition of love in a dictionary, but on the cross.*

~ JOHN STOTT ~

What can you do to increase the intimacy and depth of your love for God and others?

# He died for you

*But God demonstrates his own love for us in this: While we were still sinners, Christ died for us.*

~ ROMANS 5:8 ~

God demonstrated His love for us in that He gave His only Son to die in our place, so that, if we believe in Him, we will live forever. Because Jesus was prepared to die for you while you were still a sinner, He made it possible for you to receive the gift of God's grace. He paid the full price for your sins on the cross. And He now asks you to love each person who crosses your path in life with that same love. Will you do so?

*Love is always practical, or it is not love. Love is love because it has hands, and feet, and a mouth.*

~ JAN VAN DER WATT ~

In what ways can you show others the love of God?

# Don't delay

*For he says, "In the time of my favor I heard you, and in the day of salvation I helped you." I tell you, now is the time of God's favor, now is the day of salvation.*

~ 2 Corinthians 6:2 ~

God offers His grace to you as a free gift. But His grace can come to an end. Not one of us knows exactly how long we will live. Therefore, if you have not yet done so, today is the right time to respond to God's offer of love. Do not let the opportunity slip through your fingers. Don't delay in accepting God's gift of grace – tomorrow might be too late.

*Just as the earth can produce no fruit unless it has been fed by the sun, so can we do nothing without the grace of God.*

~ Vianney ~

Have you accepted God's gift of grace?

# *Giving brings joy*

*"In everything I did, I showed you that by this kind of hard work we must help the weak, remembering the words the Lord Jesus himself said: 'It is more blessed to give than to receive.'"*

~ Acts 20:35 ~

It is more blessed to give than to receive, says the proverb. And those who are prepared to share their possessions with others have already discovered how true it is. Giving definitely brings more joy than receiving. When you give someone a gift and you see her face light up with joy, it thrills your heart too.

God gave His Son to you, and Jesus gave His life for you. What will you give Him?

*No one can give his fellowman*
*something that he himself does not have.*
~ C. de Villiers ~

What are you prepared to give to God and others?

# The gift of life

*Enjoy life with your wife, whom you love, all the days of this ... life that God has given you under the sun.*

~ ECCLESIASTES 9:9 ~

It is wonderful to be alive. To taste God's grace and goodness each day. To love others and to be loved by others and God. We should never become blasé about the wonders of life.

Life is a gift from the hand of God that you can enjoy abundantly every day. He wants your year to be filled with joy and gladness and He wants you to delight in the people whom you love every day.

*A mundane life can be filled with adventure when it is yielded to God.*

~ PAUL TOURNIER ~

How can your life become filled with adventure this year?

# FEBRUARY

February 1

# *Joyful day*

*O my Strength, I sing praise to you; you,*
*O God, are my fortress, my loving God.*

~ Psalm 59:17 ~

My husband loves to say that a day begun with a song of praise is a day filled with sunshine. How can you go through life and not be aware of the joy it offers if you begin each day by praising God for everything that He does for you and gives to you?

That is why you should try to begin each day with a song of praise. Find something new to praise God for every day. Then each day will be a day on which you are conscious that God Himself is by your side. A day filled with joy begins with a song of joy to God.

*Jesus loves me this I know, for the Bible tells me so.*

~ Chorus ~

Write your own personal psalm of praise to God.

Father I thank You for who You are and for what You've done. I praise Your name that enables me to call upon You in my times of distress & need. I thank You for what You've done in my life & my family's life. Blessed be Your name You are My hope & my security.

# Trust in God

*"Because he loves me," says the Lord, "I will rescue him; I will protect him, for he acknowledges my name."*

~ Psalm 91:14 ~

God promises to send His angels to protect His children against dangers. And yet we often hear of Christians who are sick and suffering, Christians who are attacked and killed. How do we reconcile these things with God's promise of protection?

Even though we are not guaranteed freedom from danger in this world, we can still trust God for peace of mind and security every day. God is with you even in dangerous situations, even when you walk through the valley of the shadow of death.

*If God's intentions for your life are still unclear to you, hold fast to the knowledge that He will ultimately reveal the purpose of every situation He has allowed to come into your life.*

~ Oswald Chambers ~

What things are you struggling to reconcile with God's promises of protection?

# *God rewards faith*

*A stone was brought and placed over the mouth of the den, and the king sealed it ... so that Daniel's situation might not be changed.*

~ Daniel 6:17 ~

When Daniel was taken away into exile and made to work for a heathen king, he still believed in God. Three times a day he prayed to the God whom he loved. And God protected and blessed him, just as He still loves and protects each of His children today.

God rewarded Daniel's faith with a series of miracles – He delivered him out of the lions' den and his friends out of the fiery furnace. God can still perform wonders in your life, if you believe in Him and, as Daniel did, serve Him with all your heart.

*Faith sees the invisible, believes the unbelievable, and receives the impossible.*

~ C. S. Lewis ~

Write out your own definition of faith in the space provided here.

# God loves you

*"For God so loved the world that he gave his one and only Son, that whoever believes in him shall not perish but have eternal life."*

~ John 3:16 ~

John 3:16 must be the most well-known verse in the Bible. We learn it by heart when we are just tiny tots. This exceptional verse contains God's declaration of love to the world. God gives each one of us a second chance because of His love for us. The central message of the Bible can be summarized in this one statement: God loves you so much that He sent His Son to die in your place. To receive the gift of eternal life for yourself, you simply need to believe in Jesus.

*True joy is deeply rooted in the knowledge of God's presence and His unending love for you.*

What does God's love mean to you personally?

FEBRUARY 5

# Love is a decision

*Dear friends, let us love one another, for love comes from God. Everyone who loves has been born of God and knows God.*

~ 1 JOHN 4:7 ~

Of all the things that God asks His children to do, this is the most difficult: to love one another. We cannot love one another through our own efforts, let alone love others with the same love with which God loves us! The good news is that we do not have to try to do so. God makes it possible for us to love through His Holy Spirit who lives in us.

Love for God and your fellowman is never simply emotion. You can make the decision to love with God's help, and He will help you live out your decision.

*Where there is no love, you need to give love ... and then you will receive love.*

~ ST. JOHN OF THE CROSS ~

Write down some ways in which you can practically live out your love for God and others.

# Serve other people

*The greatest among you will be your servant.*

~ MATTHEW 23:11 ~

Serving other people is extremely important to Jesus. He Himself said that the Son of Man did not come to be served but to serve. And if we truly love Him we will want to follow His example: to be of service to others.

Even the most important among us need to be ready and willing to serve others. If you are prepared to serve others here on earth, then you will be great in God's eyes.

*Our investment in service to the Lord has a high rate of return. It will yield a harvest beyond our vastest expectations.*

~ JOHAN CILLIERS ~

Write down three ways in which you can serve others.

# Of eternal value

*Let him not deceive himself by trusting what is worthless, for he will get nothing in return.*

~ Job 15:31 ~

Each of us has certain things to which we attach great value. We are too easily inclined to trust ourselves and our material possessions. But, as Eliphaz pointed out to Job in his trials, all our earthly possessions and securities, which seem so important to us, are actually worth nothing.

Only those things that have eternal value should be valued by us. Spend your time and energy on things that will last forever. And trust in God alone.

*Heaven will be the endless portion of every man who has heaven in his soul.*

~ Henry Ward Beecher ~

How much heavenly security do you have?

# The love of God

*May your unfailing love rest upon us,*
*O Lord, even as we put our hope in you.*
~ PSALM 33:22 ~

The psalmist asks God to surround him with His love because his hope is in God alone. He knows that the people of God trusted Him and had experienced His protection time and time again.

Make this your prayer too. God is always worthy of your trust. Trust God and ask Him to cover you with His love. If the banner of God's love has been raised over you, you have no need to fear anything.

*God desires that I experience His covenant of love*
*as though everything He did, He did for me alone.*
~ JULIAN OF NORWICH ~

How many biblical proofs of
God's love for you can you list here?

# Trust Him

*He will be the sure foundation for your times,*
*a rich store of salvation and wisdom and knowledge;*
*the fear of the LORD is the key to this treasure.*

~ ISAIAH 33:6 ~

The prophet Isaiah tells us that God is the only One in whom we can place our trust all through our lives. God has never, since the beginning of time, left one of His children in the lurch.

As a child of God, you can face each new day with joy and peace of mind because you know for certain the God in whom you trust is worthy of your trust. You can depend on Him each day for the rest of your life. You can build your future on His wisdom and knowledge.

*What your heart clings to and where*
*your trust is placed – that is your god.*
~ MARTIN LUTHER ~

Write down one occasion when your trust in God gave you great comfort.

# He lives in you

*Even though I walk through the valley of the shadow of death, I will fear no evil, for you are with me; your rod and your staff, they comfort me.*

~ Psalm 23:4 ~

God is always personally present with each one of His children. He lives in you through His Holy Spirit and your safety is guaranteed in His hands. Therefore, you need never fear.

Even when you walk through times of deep darkness, you need not be fearful at all. Your Shepherd is by your side. He will carry you through the dark valleys. In His hands you are always safe. And on the other side of the darkness of life, He is waiting to welcome you to your eternal home.

*I now know that certain things look like disasters, but are, in fact, signs of grace.*

~ Phil Bosmans ~

Are you afraid to die? Why, or why not?

# He rejoices over you

*The Lord your God is with you, he is mighty to save.*
*He will take great delight in you, he will quiet you*
*with his love, he will rejoice over you with singing.*
~ Zephaniah 3:17 ~

One of my friends, who suffers from bouts of depression, phoned me recently to say that she had nurtured a seed of joy in her heart that whole day. "It is that verse in Zephaniah that says God delights in me – isn't that fantastic?" she exclaimed in delight.

God wants to be your Deliverer. He loves you. He is with you each and every day. But best of all, the God who created the whole world rejoices over you! That is indeed a reason to rejoice!

*God delights in you, even though He*
*knows the full extent of your sinfulness.*

Write down some of the reasons
why you delight in the Lord.

# Be thankful

*However many years a man may live, let him enjoy them all. ... Be happy, young man, while you are young, and let your heart give you joy in the days of your youth.*

~ ECCLESIASTES 11:8-9 ~

Very few of God's children truly realize how ungrateful they are. Most of us are so used to being healthy and having enough of everything, that we lose sight of the millions of people in the world who suffer lack, and who are sick and hungry.

Make counting your blessings every day part of your lifestyle. From now on, live each day with gratitude and enthusiasm: make each day a celebration because you belong to God.

*Gratefulness and contentment are closely related.*

~ T. VAN BAVEL ~

Write down as many of the blessings for which you are grateful that the space here allows.

# Remember your responsibilities

*Follow the ways of your heart and whatever your eyes see, but know that for all these things God will bring you to judgment.*

~ ECCLESIASTES 11:9 ~

Some people maintain that God is a spoilsport who wants to subject His children to dozens of rules and regulations. Nothing could be further from the truth!

God actually gives His law to us to show us how we can be truly happy. He wants us to be able to do the things that are fun and that we enjoy. There is just one condition: that we will always remember that we also have a responsibility to live holy lives, because God will hold us accountable for the way in which we live.

*He who provides for this life only, and takes no care for eternity, is wise for a moment but a fool forever.*

~ JOHN TILLOTSON ~

How can you live so that you please God?

Not to do anything that goes against
His teaching (His example!)

# Hope is meaningful

*May the God of hope fill you with all joy and peace as you trust in him, so that you may overflow with hope by the power of the Holy Spirit.*

~ ROMANS 15:13 ~

God is the source of our hope. We know that in the long run He will ensure that everything works out for our best. And His Holy Spirit that lives in us, makes this hope a reality and at the same time fills us with His joy and peace.

However badly things go for you, you can keep hoping in God. To hope is meaningful – each year spring succeeds the winter, the bright day follows the dark night, and one day, after death, you will be in heaven.

*Hold on to life! Hold on to hope!*
*The sun will rise again for you.*
~ I. L. DE VILLIERS ~

What does the word hope mean for you personally?

# Eternal life

*Praise be to the God and Father of our Lord Jesus Christ! In his great mercy he has given us new birth into a living hope through the resurrection of Jesus Christ from the dead, and into an inheritance that can never perish, spoil or fade – kept in heaven for you.*

~ 1 PETER 1:3-4 ~

Christians have an inheritance of incalculable value: the hope which God has in store for us in heaven. A hope that burns brightly, regardless of our present circumstances.

It is somewhat ironic that we spend so much time and money on our short earthly life and so little on the life that will last forever. Make a decision that from today you will give more of your time and energy to your imperishable, pure and eternal inheritance!

*Do not cling to the things of the earth;*
*there is so much of heaven to be had.*
~ UNKNOWN ~

What will you do to keep the hope
of heaven shining brightly in your life?

# Just do it

*Do not withhold good from those who deserve it, when it is in your power to act.*

~ PROVERBS 3:27 ~

As the proverb rightly says: A stitch in time saves nine. We have all been sorry many times because we have put things off until they eventually deteriorated beyond repair.

You should not put off doing a good deed that would help others, and for which you have the means, says the wise writer of Proverbs. Don't put off until tomorrow the things that you can do today – do them now, so that your deeds will underscore your faith.

*What would I do if I knew that today was to be my last on earth? I would plant a tree.*

~ MARTIN LUTHER ~

What things will you do today instead of putting them off till tomorrow?

# Do good for His sake

*"The King will reply, 'I tell you the truth, whatever you did for one of the least of these brothers of mine, you did for me.'"*

~ Matthew 25:40 ~

Each time I read this text I find myself digging in my purse for some loose coins to give to a beggar – even though I know it probably won't be used for food. I find myself wondering, "What if this man or woman is one of the 'least' that the Bible talks of?"

Treat other people the way that you would like to be treated. God regards everything that you do for others as if you were doing it – or not – for Him personally!

*The proof of our love for God is found*
*in our love for one another.*

~ Unknown ~

What did you do for Jesus today – or neglect to do?

# Be servants

*Not so with you. Instead, whoever wants to become great among you must be your servant, and whoever wants to be first must be your slave.*

~ MATTHEW 20:26-27 ~

Jesus was willing to take on the duties of a slave when He washed the feet of His disciples. How willing are you to jump in and help when other people have needs? To give some money is really easy, but to become actively involved in the needs of others is much more difficult.

God doesn't want His children to sit on the porch and watch the world go by, but to be servants. Are you prepared to get your hands dirty and to roll up your sleeves to help others?

*Far and away the best prize that life offers is*
*the chance to work hard at work worth doing.*
~ THEODORE ROOSEVELT ~

Decide where you will, in
future, not only give but also do.

# Don't be too busy

*"Martha, Martha," the Lord answered, "you are worried and upset about many things, but only one thing is needed. Mary has chosen what is better, and it will not be taken away from her."*

~ Luke 10:41-42 ~

Busy Martha probably had no idea how Jesus could think that Mary, by sitting at His feet and listening to Him speak, had chosen the better part. We too can become so busy with other things that little time remains for God.

Don't ever become so busy working for God that you don't have time to spend communicating with Him. Set aside time each day to spend alone with God.

*Make time for God – that is the*
*only sure investment you can make.*
~ Unknown ~

How much time do you spend with God each day?

# God's solutions

*"Do not be afraid. Stand firm and you will see the deliverance the LORD will bring you today. The LORD will fight for you; you need only to be still."*

~ EXODUS 14:13-14 ~

The Israelites saw no way out of the battle for power in which they were engaged with Pharaoh. But Moses looked past the annihilating forces of Egypt and saw God. And he knew that with God doing battle on their side, they would definitely be victorious.

God always fights on your side too. Not only does He give you the victory, but He can give you solutions for every one of your problems.

*Worry does not relieve tomorrow of its pain; it robs today of its strength.*

~ CORRIE TEN BOOM ~

What things prevent you from seeing the hand of God clearly in your life?

# Heaven's door

*He who has the Son has life; he who does not have the Son of God does not have life.*

~ 1 JOHN 5:12 ~

*"I am the Gate. Anyone who goes through me will be cared for – will freely go in and out, and find pasture. A thief is only there to steal and kill and destroy. I came so they can have real and eternal life, more and better life than they ever dreamed of,"* says Jesus (Jn. 10:9-10 *The Message*).

Without Jesus it is impossible to have eternal life, because He is the only door into heaven. If you want to live forever, you must believe in Jesus. Without Him eternal life is always out of reach – only He can unlock the door to heaven for you.

*Make sure that you live each day in such a way that you will not lose out on the eternal day.*

How many ways do you think there are to get to heaven?

Only 1 way!

# *Invite God in*

*"Here I am! I stand at the door and knock. If anyone hears my voice and opens the door, I will come in and eat with him, and he with me."*

~ REVELATION 3:20 ~

God really wants to come and make His home with you. That is why He knocks on the door of your heart. But the choice is yours. Only you can open the door. If you hear His voice and ask Him in, He will come in and live with you forever. That you can be certain of! And together with God, life from now on will be a constant celebration!

Don't put off opening the door of your heart and life to Him.

*Eternal life has its beginnings in our life on earth. It began for you on the day on which you surrendered your life to Jesus Christ.*

~ NINA SMIT ~

When and where did you open the door of your life to God?

When I was a very young girl.

# Jesus makes you new

*Therefore, if anyone is in Christ, he is a new creation; the old has gone, the new has come! All this is from God, who reconciled us to himself through Christ and gave us the ministry of reconciliation.*

~ 2 CORINTHIANS 5:17-18 ~

Anyone who is in Christ is a brand new person – so writes Paul to the congregation in Corinth. "A new life burgeons" as *The Message* translation puts it. And this newness of life is God's work, you have no part to play in it at all.

When you surrender your life to God, Jesus makes you into a new person – a new person with new characteristics. That means that you should begin to act differently. Live in such a way that people can see that you are a brand new person!

*Holiness is the expression of the life of Christ in us.*

~ J.W.C. WAND ~

In what ways did your life change when you gave your heart to Jesus?

# Your choice

*"But if serving the Lord seems undesirable to you, then choose for yourselves this day whom you will serve, whether the gods your forefathers served beyond the River, or the gods of the Amorites, in whose land you are living. But as for me and my household, we will serve the Lord."*

~ JOSHUA 24:15 ~

Joshua gave the people a choice: they needed to decide once and for all if they would serve the one true God or the foreign gods. With great fanfare, the people chose God – but it wasn't long before they turned away from the God whom they had chosen.

Unfortunately, the same is true of many of us. Today God gives you the chance to choose once again. The choice to allow Him into your life is your own. No one else can make the decision for you. Whom do you choose?

*The decision for or against God is the most important one you will ever make.*

Have you decided to follow Jesus?

# Glad tidings

*"But you will receive power when the Holy Spirit comes on you; and you will be my witnesses in Jerusalem, and in all Judea and Samaria, and to the ends of the earth."*

~ ACTS 1:8 ~

Jesus promised His twelve disciples that the Holy Spirit would equip them to tell other people about Him – in the communities in which they lived, in the countries in which they lived and even to the ends of the earth.

God still calls you to be His witness. How can you keep the good news of Jesus to yourself? The Holy Spirit will give you the boldness to share it with others.

*First talk to God about your friends before you talk to your friends about God.*

Do you find it easy to talk to others about your faith?

# The longer you are a Christian ...

*But grow in the grace and knowledge of our Lord and Savior Jesus Christ. To him be glory both now and forever! Amen.*

~ 2 PETER 3:18 ~

We can never stop learning more about Jesus. Through studying His Word and the way He lived His life we will learn more and more about Him. And so we discover more and more about His grace.

The longer you are a Christian, the better you will learn to know Jesus, the more you will love Him and the more His characteristics will become visible in your life. Make sure that you grow spiritually each day.

*If you want to serve God, you must be prepared to follow Him.*

Set yourself some spiritual goals. Write them down here.

# Spiritually mature

*Until we all reach unity in the faith and in the knowledge of the Son of God and become mature, attaining to the whole measure of the fullness of Christ.*

~ EPHESIANS 4:13 ~

Being spiritually mature means that you will become more and more dependent on God. Then each day you will decrease, set aside the sins of the old man and become more like Jesus in your actions. Then you will be like a fully mature person, as perfect and complete as Jesus Himself. Eventually you will be able to say, together with Paul, *"I no longer live, but Christ lives in me"* (Gal. 2:20).

*Only when you have died to your sinful nature will you begin to grow spiritually and bear fruit for God.*

What areas of your life are evidence that you are growing spiritually?

# Fruit of your labor

*For we are God's fellow workers; you are God's field, God's building. ... Always give yourselves fully to the work of the Lord, because you know that your labor in the Lord is not in vain.*

~ 1 CORINTHIANS 3:9, 15:58 ~

Each child of God is called to work for Him full time. Therefore each of us should know the hope to which we have been called and hold fast to what we believe. We should never lose our enthusiasm. If there is something that you can do for God, you should do it.

Although you often do not immediately see the fruit of your labor, what you do for the Lord is always worth the effort. Don't be tempted to become slack in your commitment to His work.

*Take a regular dose of enthusiasm – and you will find opportunities to praise God around every corner.*

~ MARCELLE AUCLAIR ~

Be honest: How enthusiastic are you concerning the things of the Lord?

# Do it for the glory of God

*So whether you eat or drink or whatever you do, do it all for the glory of God.*

~ 1 CORINTHIANS 10:31 ~

If you learn to do all that you do as if you were doing it for God Himself, it will eventually make a tremendous difference in your life. Other people will see that God comes first in your life. Your daily chores will even become much more pleasant for you when you do them to the glory of God. Ask the Lord to bless your work. And make absolutely certain that you do nothing that will harm or damage other people.

*Do your work as if you are working for God Himself – and see what positive changes occur in your life.*

List your tasks for the day. Ask God to help you do them to the best of your ability.

# March

# Be strong and courageous!

*Say to those with fearful hearts, "Be strong, do not fear; your God will come, he will come with vengeance; with divine retribution he will come to save you."*

~ ISAIAH 35:4 ~

It is not unusual these days to meet many people who want to throw in the towel because of all the negative things that happen around them. The prophet Isaiah has a message of comfort for such people: God Himself says to them that they must be strong, and that they need fear nothing because He is with them.

If you are sitting in the depths of despair today, you can be strong and courageous. God knows about each one of your problems, and puts His strength at your disposal. And because He is with you, daily crises need never get the better of you.

*The very act of hoping produces a kind of strength of its own.*

~ NORMAN VINCENT PEALE ~

What things discourage you?

# Sleep in peace

*I will not fear the tens of thousands drawn up against me on every side.*

~ Psalm 3:6 ~

The writer of Psalm 3 has a very positive testimony. He does not have to lie awake all night, tossing and turning while mulling over his problems. He sleeps peacefully each night and wakes up worry free because of the assurance that the Lord cares for Him and strengthens him. Therefore he can handle any crises in his life.

Does worry sometimes keep you awake at night? From now on you can sleep in peace: your God can and will provide for your every need!

*When you lie awake at night, don't count sheep. Talk to the Shepherd instead.*

~ Unknown ~

If you are anxious, ask God to calm your thoughts and give you peaceful rest.

# Peaceful oasis

*My soul finds rest in God alone; my salvation comes from him. He alone is my rock and my salvation; he is my fortress, I will never be shaken.*

~ Psalm 62:1-2 ~

The world today is beset by a spirit of restlessness. But Christians have a peace that comes from deep within because they can trust in God at all times. He delivers us in times of need, and is our source of strength when things get too much for us to handle.

God wants to be your oasis of peace in a chaotic world. You can always find help and refuge in Him. All that you need to do is to trust Him.

*Faith arrays itself against anxiety, and that is why we need to learn to trust in this life.*

~ Johan Heyns ~

Do you find yourself stressing too easily, or are you able to trust God in everything?

# God protects

*You hem me in – behind and before; you have laid your hand upon me.*

~ Psalm 139:5 ~

God surrounds His children: He goes before them to show them the way, beside them to help them along their journey through life, behind them to protect them from dangers, and above them to pour out His blessings on them.

Even if you face dangers every day, God still hems you in on all sides. He will protect and keep you. Nothing that can do you lasting harm can penetrate the shield of His protection that surrounds His children.

*God always protects His children – even death will bring us safely to His presence in heaven.*

In what areas do you need God's protection?

# Anchored in faith

*Give thanks in all circumstances, for this is God's will for you in Christ Jesus.*

~ 1 Thessalonians 5:18 ~

God doesn't just ask His children to be thankful, but to be thankful in all things, including those things that they would have liked to have been different: the things that cause them pain and the things that they cannot understand.

The secret of the Christian's thankfulness is that it does not depend on his circumstances, but is anchored in his faith.

*Gratefulness is a virtue that can be learned.*

Are you able to thank God even for the things you wish had been different?

# God's love for you

*He replied, "You give them something to eat." They answered, "We have only five loaves of bread and two fish – unless we go and buy food for all this crowd."*

~ Luke 9:13 ~

When Jesus' disciples asked Him where they were to get enough food to feed the thousands of hungry people who had been listening to Him, they received a surprising answer: He told them that they should find food because it was their responsibility to care for the crowds.

God expects you to minister to the needs of the less privileged around you. What you do for Christ is the mirror in which others can see the love of God in your life – and your love for Him.

*True love begins when you truly expect nothing in return.*

~ Antoine de Saint-Exupery ~

What are you doing so that others can see the love of God in your life?

# Your love for God

*"And if anyone gives even a cup of cold water to one of these little ones because he is my disciple, I tell you the truth, he will certainly not lose his reward."*

~ Matthew 10:42 ~

If you truly love God, then you will also love other people and their needs will touch your heart, compelling you to do something to help them. When we help those who have less than we do, we indirectly help God and He will reward us.

The extent of your love for God is measured in the way in which you treat other people – especially those who are unable to return any favors.

*To have and not to give what you have is worse than to steal.*

~ Marie van Ebner-Eschenbach ~

Today, do something good for someone who does not deserve it.

# A free gift

*"But love your enemies, do good to them, and lend to them without expecting to get anything back. Then your reward will be great, and you will be sons of the Most High, because he is kind to the ungrateful and wicked."*

~ LUKE 6:35 ~

Jesus asks those who follow Him to love their enemies and do good to them, without expecting anything in return. It is very hard to get this right, but those who do manage it will receive a great reward: they will be called children of God.

If you do something for someone else, it should be freely given, not something that will somehow be of advantage to you. And then God Himself will reward you for it.

*Loving means to love that which is unlovable – or it is no virtue at all.*

~ GILBERT KEITH CHESTERTON ~

Write down the names of two people you don't really like, and begin to pray for them regularly.

# Your own sins

*"Why do you look at the speck of sawdust in your brother's eye and pay no attention to the plank in your own eye?"*

~ LUKE 6:41 ~

People are inclined to look at their own sins through dark glasses, and the sins of others through the lens of a microscope. When you do something wrong it is never really bad in your own eyes, but if someone else were to do the exact same thing, you would probably find it unforgivable.

Make an effort from now on to treat other people as you would like them to treat you, and judge them in the same way that you would like to be judged.

*Only God has the right to throw the first stone – but He never does.*

~ XHOSA PREACHER ~

What things do you do, but are quick to criticize in others?

# Sweep your own front porch

*"How can you say to your brother, 'Brother, let me take the speck out of your eye,' when you yourself fail to see the plank in your own eye? You hypocrite, first take the plank out of your eye, and then you will see clearly to remove the speck from your brother's eye."*

~ LUKE 6:42 ~

People who have double standards are nothing more than hypocrites. Look carefully at your own faults, and do what you can to put them right. Only then will you have the right to address the faults of others. At the same time you will learn to be more understanding of their weaknesses. Not one of us is without fault!

In other words, sweep your own front porch before you check to see if your neighbor's yard is clean.

*To err is human; to forgive, divine.*

~ ALEXANDER POPE ~

Make a list of some of your worst faults.
How will you begin to change them?

# Put your hand in the hand of Jesus

*But when he saw the wind, he was afraid and, beginning to sink, cried out, "Lord, save me!" Immediately Jesus reached out his hand and caught him. "You of little faith," he said, "why did you doubt?"*

~ Matthew 14:30-31 ~

When Peter saw that he was going to sink under the waves, he called to Jesus to help him. And Jesus was immediately ready to reach out a helping hand. But, He still admonished Peter for his lack of faith.

If it seems as though you are drowning in the sea of your circumstances, put your hand in Jesus' hand – He will deliver you from trouble every time. But make sure that you have faith and believe that He will do so.

*Courage for the great heartaches life brings;*
*patience with the small annoyances – this too is faith.*

~ Victor Hugo ~

How do you handle crises in your life?

# Spiritually fit

*Consider it pure joy, my brothers, whenever you face trials of many kinds, because you know that the testing of your faith develops perseverance. Perseverance must finish its work so that you may be mature and complete, not lacking anything.*

~ James 1:2-4 ~

Not one of us likes our faith to be tested through times of suffering, but hard times provide good exercise for Christians. They increase our faith. Negative things in our lives test how much we really trust God, and teach us to live closer to Him.

Hard times are never pleasant, but they exercise your faith, making you spiritually fit – through hard times your faith gets stronger and you learn to persevere.

*There are no crown-wearers in heaven*
*who were not cross-bearers here below.*
~ Charles Spurgeon ~

Write down two benefits of suffering and affliction.

Spiritual growth - i.e. getting closer to God. Our faith improves - we trust Him

# He will carry you

*There you saw how the Lord your God carried you, as a father carries his son, all the way you went until you reached this place.*

~ Deuteronomy 1:31 ~

God was physically present with His people during all their years of wondering in the wilderness: as a cloud by day and a pillar of fire by night. He provided for every one of their needs.

God is still with His children each day, and He will carry us when we feel we cannot go any further. God goes ahead of you on your path through life. He will provide for every one of your needs and carry you through areas in your life when problems get you down and you feel you cannot go on.

*To have faith is to have wings.*

~ J. M. Barrie ~

Where and when has God carried you when you were unable to walk?

# Your relationship with the Lord

*"If you keep your feet from breaking the Sabbath and from doing as you please on my holy day, if you call the Sabbath a delight and the Lord's holy day honorable, ... then you will find your joy in the Lord, and I will cause you to ride on the heights of the land and to feast on the inheritance of your father Jacob."*

~ ISAIAH 58:13-14 ~

There are very few modern day Christians who treat Sundays the way God prescribes in His Word. What do you do on Sundays?

What you do on Sundays should be an indication of your relationship with the Lord. It is the one day in the week that you should set aside for Him and not focus on other things. If you do this, you will find joy in His presence.

*I feel as if God had, by giving the Sabbath, given fifty-two springs in every year.*
~ SAMUEL TAYLOR COLERIDGE ~

Is Sunday a special day set apart for the Lord, or just another ordinary day for you?

# *God is able to help*

*Surely the arm of the Lord is not too short to save, nor his ear too dull to hear.*

~ Isaiah 59:1 ~

During the Exile, the people of God were constantly reminded of His promises, which He constantly renewed. He promised to help and rescue them in spite of the fact that they had so often turned away from Him.

God is just the same today as He was during Bible days. He still wants to help His children and listen to their problems. Even if your problems are beyond human help and your difficulties insurmountable, God is able to help. Nothing is impossible for Him.

*Faith gives the courage to take risks beyond what can be seen.*

~ W. N. Clark ~

In what areas do you need God's help today?

# Jesus conquered death

*When the perishable has been clothed with the imperishable, and the mortal with immortality, then the saying that is written will come true: "Death has been swallowed up in victory." But thanks be to God! He gives us the victory through our Lord Jesus Christ.*

~ 1 Corinthians 15:54, 57 ~

Most people are fearful of dying – possibly because death is such an unknown entity. When Jesus rose from the dead, He was able to put an end to the fear of death. He took the sting out of death's tail, said Paul.

You need, therefore, no longer be afraid of death. Jesus has already conquered death. Death for you is simply stepping into the Father's House where you will live happily together with Jesus forever.

*Live in such a way that you need never fear death.*

Can you honestly say that you are not afraid to die?

MARCH 17

# Give a smile!

*All the days of the oppressed are wretched,*
*but the cheerful heart has a continual feast.*

~ PROVERBS 15:15 ~

Some people go through life with long faces. They find nothing beautiful or pleasant around them. And things seem to go wrong for them all the time. Thankfully, there are also the joyful people who find something in each day that they can be glad about. And life is a continual feast for such people, as the wise writer of Proverbs pointed out.

Make sure that you are a cheerful person. Keep a lookout for the things in each day that can bring you joy – and if you should see someone without a smile, give him one of yours!

*The more we find the source of joy*
*within our hearts, the happier we will be.*

~ SCHOPENHAUER ~

What things make you glad? Write them down!

M - News from the children, spiritual commitment
- Good health
- A loving family
- Friends

# *God is wonderful*

*"Be still, and know that I am God."*
~ PSALM 46:10 ~

No one seems to have enough time these days – no time for themselves, no time for each other, and no time for God. Our lives are one hectic mad rush from one appointment to another, from one commitment to another – and all the while we become spiritually poorer.

The time has come to slow down. Set aside at least half an hour a day to be quiet before God. Meditate on His wonder and might and praise Him for His grace and mercy toward you.

*The most valuable part of any day*
*is the time spent alone with God.*

Set aside an extra ten minutes for your quiet time today.

# You are precious

*Since you are precious and honored in my sight, and because I love you, I will give men in exchange for you, and people in exchange for your life.*

~ Isaiah 43:4 ~

It is easy to develop an inferiority complex if you keep comparing yourself to friends who are prettier, thinner, and more talented than you are. In the process you quickly forget how highly God regards you. He Himself says that He loves you, that He thinks highly of you, that He has made you in His image and that He knows your name.

When you feel as if no one respects you, remember that God sees you as eternally precious.

*When you look at yourself through God's eyes, you will rid yourself of your inferiority complex forever.*

Write a positive description of yourself.

# Friendship is precious

*A man of many companions may come to ruin, but there is a friend who sticks closer than a brother.*

~ Proverbs 18:24 ~

It sometimes happens that people whom we trust betray our trust. If you have ever been hurt in this way, it becomes more difficult to trust other people the next time. But then you discover that there are friends who will never let you down. They never disappoint you, and are always there when you need them.

Friendship is precious. Treasure the friends that you have, and nurture them. And always remember: before you can have a friend, you need to be a friend.

*A friend is the most powerful comfort in every need.*

~ Phil Bosmans ~

Write down the names of your best friends and make a commitment to pray for them daily.

# Jesus will never leave you

*Greater love has no one than this, that he lay down his life for his friends. You are my friends if you do what I command.*

~ John 15:13-14 ~

There is no one who is perfect. Therefore you can count on it that even your best friend will let you down at times. Jesus, however, is the one Friend who will always be with you, who will never disappoint you and who will never leave you, who loves you so much that He even gave His life so that you can live.

And today He comes to you to tell you that you can be His friend, if you are prepared do the things that He asks in His Word.

*Jesus will always be the best friend you could ever have. Base your friendships on His example.*

What is the best thing you have ever done for one of your friends?

# God will carry you

*"You yourselves have seen what I did to Egypt, and how I carried you on eagles' wings and brought you to myself."*

~ Exodus 19:4 ~

God led His people safely through the wilderness. He uses the image of an eagle and its young to describe His protective love of His people. Just as an eagle flies beneath its young to prevent them from falling while they are learning to fly, God will carry His people safely on eagle's wings.

This promise is directed at you too: God will protect you today, and He wants to carry you through the hard times just as an eagle carries its young.

*Dear Lord, look after Yourself, for if something should happen to You, we would not survive.*

~ Children's Prayer ~

Let go and let God!

# Your enthusiasm might wane

*Never be lacking in zeal, but keep your spiritual fervor, serving the Lord.*
~ Romans 12:11 ~

When you are newly born again, you are usually enthusiastic for the things of the Lord. Nothing is too much trouble for you. You set aside much time for your personal devotions, you go to church often, and you pray without ceasing. Sometimes this early dedication diminishes, but it should not.

It is a typical human reaction for the initial enthusiasm for the things of the Lord to lessen. Make sure that this does not happen to you.

*Enthusiasm is the dynamism of love. Do everything with a smile on your lips and a song in your heart.*
~ Kathleen Keating ~

Are you as enthusiastic and passionate about God as you were when you were first born again?

March 24

# Your life should change

*All Scripture is God-breathed and is useful for teaching, rebuking, correcting and training in righteousness.*

~ 2 Timothy 3:16 ~

The Bible has a deep influence on your whole life. It helps you to help others who have wandered from God's path; it helps you to discern between what is right and wrong; it also teaches you how God expects you to live and what He expects from you.

Therefore, it is not enough simply to have a good knowledge of Biblical facts. The Word of God should change your life for the better. Live as the Bible asks you to!

*In all my perplexities and distresses the Bible has never failed to give me light and strength.*

~ Robert E. Lee ~

How much time do you set aside to read the Bible every day?

# The Holy Spirit as teacher

*I keep asking that the God of our Lord Jesus Christ, the glorious Father, may give you the Spirit of wisdom and revelation, so that you may know him better.*

~ Ephesians 1:17 ~

When you open the Bible, God will speak personally to you, and He sends His Holy Spirit to explain the Scriptures to you. The Spirit of God gives you the necessary wisdom so that you can understand the Word.

Without the Holy Spirit teaching you, you will not be able to fully grasp the message of the Bible. He is the only Person who can give you real insight into God's Word. Ask Him now to help you when you read the Bible.

*First pray that the Holy Spirit will open the Bible to you before you open it.*

Have you seen the Holy Spirit reveal Bible truths to you?

# God's Word

*Let the word of Christ dwell in you richly as you teach and admonish one another with all wisdom, and as you sing psalms, hymns and spiritual songs with gratitude in your hearts to God.*

~ COLOSSIANS 3:16 ~

Every word in the Bible comes from God Himself. Therefore, you should never be satisfied until you know everything that He wants you to know. Study the Bible so that you can really know what it says. Make time to study the Bible in depth, using concordances and different Bible translations.

If you also make the effort to learn key passages by heart, you will always have God's Word with you, and it will become a precious, inextricable part of your life.

*God's Word shows us the best way to live, the most noble way to suffer and the only way to die in peace.*
~ JOHN FLAVEL ~

Try to memorize at least one Bible verse each week.

# God's law

*And God spoke all these words ... Teach them the decrees and laws, and show them the way to live and the duties they are to perform.*

~ Exodus 20:1, 18:20 ~

Some people do not like the Ten Commandments. They think they are a set of stifling rules and regulations that God has instituted to keep them in check. Nothing could be further from the truth. God's law is the road map that He provides for His children. It helps you to know what road to follow if you want to live a life of true joy.

Spend some time looking at God's commandments again, allowing them to point out the road for you to travel.

*The Law is not a prerequisite for our becoming God's children, but a guideline to show us how to live as children of God.*

~ Johan Smit ~

Can you write down all Ten Commandments, without looking them up?

# Nothing is as important as God

*"I am the Lord your God, who brought you out of Egypt, out of the land of slavery. You shall have no other gods before me."*

~ Exodus 20:2-3 ~

God does not tolerate His people turning from Him to worship idols. He wants you to serve Him only. He wants to be your only God. Even though He regularly renewed His covenant of love with His people, they still often turned from Him to worship foreign gods.

Even though we no longer worship statues of gods, anything that is more important in our lives than God Himself is an idol. Make sure that there is nothing in your life that means more than your relationship with God.

*Anything that is more important to you than God is an idol.*

Write down things in your life that are more important to you than God. Be honest.

# God is almighty

*The earth is the Lord's, and everything in it, the world, and all who live in it.*

~ Psalm 24:1 ~

God is the Creator of all things. He created the world and all that is in it, He maintains it day by day, and therefore the earth and everything in it belongs to God.

The God you worship is almighty. He can do all things. Everything around you belongs to Him. And even though you live in a world of unrest and violence, your future, and that of your children, is safe in His hands.

*I have never understood how anyone could look at a baby, a flower or a sunset and not believe in God.*

Take time to watch the sun set, and describe the beauty you see.

# Love and fear

*There is no fear in love. But perfect love drives out fear, because fear has to do with punishment. The one who fears is not made perfect in love.*

~ 1 JOHN 4:18 ~

It is impossible to love God and to trust Him and yet still be afraid and worried about many things. If you love God above all things, there will not be place in your life for fear to get a foothold.

Make a list of all the things of which you are afraid, the things that cause you stress and the things that you are worried about and then give the list to God. Love and fear cannot exist side by side.

*Half of what we fear has no basis, the other half has no faith.*

~ CHRISTIAN BOVÉE ~

Are you able to exchange your fears for God's peace?

# With Jesus at your side

*I can do everything through*
*him who gives me strength.*
~ Philippians 4:13 ~

Paul was an exceptional man who attempted unbelievable things. The reason he could do what he did is explained in Philippians 4:13: he could literally do all things because God gave him the strength to get them right.

Jesus wants to be a source of strength for you today and His strength is at your disposal. Be strong and courageous: if He is with you, there is absolutely nothing that you and He together cannot do.

*All joy has two basic ingredients: courage and hard work.*
~ Honoré de Balzac ~

What would you, with God, still like to achieve?

Learn another language

# APRIL

April 1

# God has no favorites

*And masters, treat your slaves in the same way. Do not threaten them, since you know that he who is both their Master and yours is in heaven, and there is no favoritism with him.*

~ Ephesians 6:9 ~

Sometimes, unintentionally, we feel that God favors other people over us – people who are better than us. But that cannot be, affirms Paul to the church at Ephesus. We all worship the same God, and God has no favorites. He treats each one of His children in exactly the same way.

Take Paul's words to heart and make sure that you don't favor some people above others. Try to treat everyone with whom you come into contact in exactly the same way.

*God is absolutely fair and just. He treats each one of His millions of children in exactly the same way.*

Do you have favorites? What can you do to try not to show favoritism?

# God is our Rock

*The Lord is a refuge for the oppressed,*
*a stronghold in times of trouble.*

~ PSALM 9:9 ~

When we turn on the TV or open a newspaper, it seems that danger is all around us. People are robbed, assaulted and murdered. We don't feel safe anywhere. And so we live behind fences and walls and are sometimes afraid even to open our front doors.

But God is still a Rock for His children to which they can flee in times of trouble, just as He was when the psalmist wrote these words – He can protect you from any danger.

*That I fear is not a matter of concern, but when I do not learn from my fear, then I should begin to worry.*

~ JOHAN HEYNS ~

What fears do you still need to unburden at the feet of Christ?

# Wait for His answer

*My heart is not proud, O Lord, my eyes are not haughty; I do not concern myself with great matters or things too wonderful for me. But I have stilled and quieted my soul; like a weaned child with its mother, like a weaned child is my soul within me.*

~ Psalm 131:1-2 ~

There are many things that happen to us that we cannot understand. We have dozens of "why?" questions that don't receive any answers. But it isn't always necessary for us to understand the way God acts. God's children do not need to tire themselves out over things that they do not understand. They can rest safely in God's arms and wait for His answers. Do this next time you are looking for answers.

*You can trust God to lead you on the path that is, for you, the best way to travel through this world.*
~ Unknown ~

Write down some of the things that you need to trust to God's care.

# God always answers

*When I called, you answered me; you made me bold and stouthearted.*
~ Psalm 138:3 ~

When we pray God will answer – but sometimes He answers in His own time and in His own way, and that means that sometimes His answer is not what we would have chosen it to be.

If you have been praying for a long time about an issue and do not yet have an answer, keep on praying. God is there, and He hears you. He will answer your prayer and give you the strength you need as you wait for the answer. Rest in His answer – it is the right one for you.

*I have lived to thank God that all of*
*my prayers have not been answered.*
~ Jean Ingelow ~

In what ways has God answered your prayers?

# Serenity

*Therefore my heart is glad and my tongue rejoices; my body also will rest secure. You have made known to me the path of life; you will fill me with joy in your presence, with eternal pleasures at your right hand.*

~ PSALM 16:9, 11 ~

As Christians, we can live with serenity and a song in our hearts. We are always safe because we trust in God; we rejoice in the grace and in the guidance that He gives us in our lives. It is when we are close to Him that we are filled with joy.

You too can live with peace in your heart and leave your problems in God's hands.

*You may trust the Lord too little,*
*but you can never trust Him too much.*

~ ANONYMOUS ~

Are you in the place where you can trust every aspect of your life to God's care?

# God is always the same

*Jesus Christ is the same yesterday and today and forever.*

~ Hebrews 13:8 ~

Each day we see how things around us change. Technology, science, politics, the economy and world opinions. The truth is that we can be absolutely certain of nothing. Except God. He is exactly the same yesterday, today and for all time. He is the only One who cannot change. Therefore, you don't need to learn to trust God anew each day. He is always the same. He has proved His faithfulness in the past.

*God is, and all is well.*

~ John Greenleaf Whittier ~

What things have changed dramatically in your life in the last ten years?

# Hard times

*This poor man called, and the Lord heard him; he saved him out of all his troubles.*

~ PSALM 34:6 ~

Many times God uses your difficulties as a platform from which you can bear testimony of His goodness. It is more difficult to trust God and rejoice in Him during hard times than when things are going well. But God makes it possible for us to be filled with His joy even in the midst of troubles. You can rejoice because God holds you in the palm of His hand and you know for sure that He will help you now, just as He has always done in the past.

*Suffering only becomes meaningful when we discover that it can lead us to honor God.*

~ JOHAN SMIT ~

In what ways has suffering in your life ultimately benefited you?

# True Joy

*Blessed is the man who does not walk in the counsel of the wicked or stand in the way of sinners or sit in the seat of mockers. But his delight is in the law of the Lord, and on his law he meditates day and night.*

~ Psalm 1:1-2 ~

When you open your Bible you meet God Himself and He gives you His joy. God's children find joy when they are assured of His love and mercy in His Word, and time after time hear His voice speaking personally to them as they read it.

The secret of true joy is to find your joy in the Word of God, rather than in the pleasures of this world.

*Seek God's will where He has spoken – in His Word.*

~ Johan Smit ~

In what areas does your faith bring you the most joy?

# Possessions

*Better what the eye sees*
*than the roving of the appetite.*
~ Ecclesiastes 6:9 ~

Material security is a topic that is focused on with much pressure these days. But money and possessions cannot guarantee your happiness. To be happy is to be satisfied with the things that you have. To know for certain that you have a heavenly Father who can see to your every need.

If your happiness is dependent on your possessions, you will never have enough. Value and enjoy the things that you do have, rather than desiring more.

*Those who are rich are no happier than*
*those who have enough for their needs.*
~ Solon ~

Honestly assess how important money and possessions are to you.

# *Work is a privilege*

*Then I realized that it is good and proper for a man to eat and drink, and to find satisfaction in his toilsome labor under the sun during the few days of life God has given him – for this is his lot.*

~ Ecclesiastes 5:18 ~

Sometimes we complain that the amount of work we have to do keeps us busy for hours. But work is satisfying and enriching. To be able to work is a privilege. The ability to be able to work, as well as the enthusiasm to do your work joyfully, are gifts from God.

If you have a job that allows you to use your talents, do it as if you were doing it for God and remember to work with joy in your heart. Your work is a gift from God.

*Set me a task in which I can put something of my very self, and it is a task no longer; it is joy; it is art.*

~ Bliss Carman ~

Do you enjoy your work? Why or why not?

# Use today

*Do not say, "Why were the old days better than these?" For it is not wise to ask such questions.*

~ Ecclesiastes 7:10 ~

Some people long nostalgically for the past when everything, according to them, was so much better than now. They are never satisfied with anything in the present. Neither the social conditions, the cost of living nor the political situation.

If you are one of those people who long for "the good old days", you need to make a paradigm shift. Guard against always living in the past. That is foolishness, says the preacher. Set your hope on the future and use today to really live life to the full.

*Yesterday is a canceled check; tomorrow is a promissory note; today is cash! Use it wisely!*
~ Barbara Johnson ~

Do you often find yourself longing for the "good old days"?

# Use every opportunity

*Whatever your hand finds to do, do it with all your might.*

~ Ecclesiastes 9:10 ~

Each day dozens of opportunities come your way. Sometimes you are too tired and sometimes just too lazy to grab hold of them, and so you let them slip past you – only to be sorry later that you did so. Learn to live in such a way that you get the most out of life.

Make the most of every opportunity that comes your way, work hard, and enjoy it – you might never again get the chance that you waste today.

*Make sure that where you invest your energy has true and lasting value.*

~ Dirk Guelpa ~

What do you spend most of your time doing?

# Faith brings results

*That is why I did not even consider myself worthy to come to you. But say the word, and my servant will be healed. When Jesus heard this, he was amazed at him, and turning to the crowd following him, he said, "I tell you, I have not found such great faith even in Israel."*

~ LUKE 7:7, 9 ~

When people come to Jesus with requests and supplications, He first looks to see if they really believe that He can do the things that they ask of Him. And if He sees that they believe in His power, then He gladly grants their requests.

Do you believe that God can answer your prayers? Faith always brings results. And a strong faith is never your own doing – it is a response to the greatness of God.

*Faith is not doing something. It is to stop doing and to allow God to rescue you.*

~ FLIP THERON ~

What does faith mean to you?

# Faith saves

*For in Christ Jesus neither circumcision nor uncircumcision has any value. The only thing that counts is faith expressing itself through love.*

~ GALATIANS 5:6 ~

When you become a Christian, your life changes. You are now a new person. What should be important to you now is that your faith will be made evident by the things that you do in love for others.

You are saved by faith, but once you are saved, you demonstrate your faith in the things that you do – then the great deeds that God asks of you will follow – as an offering of thanks for the fact that God has saved you.

*What I want is, not to possess religion*
*but to have a religion that shall possess me.*

~ CHARLES KINGSLEY ~

What things do you do differently
because you believe in God?

# Offer of grace

*For their sake he remembered his covenant*
*and out of his great love he relented.*
~ Psalm 106:45 ~

We read in many places in the Old Testament how God demonstrated His covenant to His disobedient nation. Because He loved them, He was always ready to help them.

At the baptismal font God offers you His covenant of grace. But you need to respond personally to this offer of grace. Have you done so? If you have, He will also be prepared to forgive your sins and to show by His grace how much He loves you.

*Fortunate are those who know that*
*discipleship is simply a life that flows from grace ...*
*And this grace simply means discipleship.*
~ Dietrich Bonhoeffer ~

What does your baptism mean to you?

# True faith

*He withdrew about a stone's throw beyond them, knelt down and prayed, "Father, if you are willing, take this cup from me; yet not my will, but yours be done."*

~ Luke 22:41-42 ~

In Gethsemane Jesus prayed so earnestly for God to remove the cup of suffering from Him, that His sweat fell like drops of blood to the ground. Because He was completely human, He could not see His way clear to endure the inhuman suffering that was awaiting Him. Yet He was willing to rest in His Father's will.

True faith means seeking God's will in prayer, not forcing your opinion on Him.

*Before you can fully obey God's will,*
*you need to surrender your own will.*

Are you prepared to end all your prayers as Jesus ended His in Gethsemane?

April 17

# Hope

*But if we hope for what we do not yet have, we wait for it patiently.*

~ Romans 8:25 ~

We like to say that seeing is believing. But God wants His children to hope in those things that they cannot yet see. He wants them to be so certain of His promises that they will hold fast to them, even though they have not yet seen them come to fulfillment.

Hope is the steadfast trust that the things that you desire will one day be a reality. And you will never be ashamed when you hope in God. Persevere in hope!

*Hope is patience that has lighted its lamp at God's light.*

~ Tertullian ~

Which of your dreams would
you most like to see come to pass?

# God's promises

*The Lord is good to those whose hope*
*is in him, to the one who seeks him.*

~ Lamentations 3:25 ~

For the person who lives in hope, the future is full of promise – the promise that God's promises will come to pass. And Christians have the assurance that there is a future for them in heaven with God. That all the difficulties of the present will be done away with forever, and that only the joy of God will remain. The new heaven and the new earth that God has promised will be a reality for them.

*In all circumstances it is better to hope than to despair.*
*Who can determine what is or is not possible?*

~ Goethe ~

Write down some of the verses from
Peter's sermon on this topic. (1 Pet. 1:3-9)

# Glory in heaven

*Be joyful in hope, patient in affliction, faithful in prayer.*

~ Romans 12:12 ~

Paul encouraged the Christians in Rome to look forward with joy to the day when God will make all things new, not to lose hope in hard times, and not to stop praying.

Make it your resolution this year to live in hope and to cling to God in times of crisis. Christians can endure hard times far better than unbelievers because they live with hope in their hearts – the hope of glory that awaits them in heaven.

*As long as there is hope, only the cowardly give up.*

~ Bertrand Russell ~

Can you hold on to hope when things go wrong?

# God knows about your problems

*Why do you say, O Jacob, and complain, O Israel, "My way is hidden from the Lord; my cause is disregarded by my God"? ... The Lord is the everlasting God, the Creator of the ends of the earth. He will not grow tired or weary, and his understanding no one can fathom. But those who hope in the Lord will renew their strength.*

~ Isaiah 40:27, 28, 31 ~

Sometimes when we go through really difficult times it seems as if God has forgotten about us. Thankfully, that is impossible. God is almighty. There is nothing that He does not know about. Even if you feel that He does not know what is happening, be assured that He does know everything that makes life difficult for you.

Therefore, hold on to hope. God knows about each one of your problems. He sees your pain and offers you His love and help.

*God washes our eyes with tears until we see the unseen country where He Himself will wipe every tear from our eyes.*
~ Henry Ward Beecher ~

What are you looking forward to in heaven?

# Find your joy in the Lord

*Delight yourself in the Lord and he will give you the desires of your heart. Commit your way to the Lord; trust in him and he will do this.*

~ Psalm 37:4-5 ~

People who live far from God try in vain to find joy in life. There are just too many negative things that make them despondent and tense. But for those who trust in God, joy is a way of life. They discover from day to day that God fulfills all their desires and gives them things that they don't really need but that make life more pleasant.

Find your joy in the Lord. Yield your life to Him, trust in Him and He will give you the desires of your heart.

*There is no greater joy or comfort than knowing, in the midst of your troubles, that you are surrounded by the love of God.*

~ John Calvin ~

Can other people see the joy of God on your face?

# Smilers

*The ransomed of the Lord will return. They will enter Zion with singing; everlasting joy will crown their heads. Gladness and joy will overtake them, and sorrow and sighing will flee away.*

~ Isaiah 35:10 ~

Isaiah prophesied that the people who were taken away, weeping, into exile would return to Zion as people filled with joy. And it is the Lord who makes their return from exile, as well as their joy, possible.

God still wants to make His children happy. The secret of people who are always smiling is that they have Jesus in their lives. The joy that He gives cannot be hidden away: it radiates happiness all around.

*We cannot find peace and joy apart from God because, quite simply, there is no joy without God.*

~ C. S. Lewis ~

Does it give you great joy to know you belong to God? Why?

# God's promises

*Not one of all the Lord's good promises to the house of Israel failed; every one was fulfilled.*

~ Joshua 21:45 ~

Joshua assured the people that God always does what He has promised. Not even one of His promises can remain unfulfilled. Every promise will come to fruition.

There are some things God cannot do! He cannot ever be untrue to one of His promises. You can believe with your whole heart that every promise God made in His Word, that pertains to you, will come to pass if you believe in Him, just as it did for His people long ago.

*I believe in the sun even if it does not shine.*
*I believe in God even if I do not see Him.*
~ Hans Kung ~

Write down some of God's promises that have come to pass in your life.

# Faith and trust

*Therefore I tell you, whatever you ask for in prayer, believe that you have received it, and it will be yours.*

~ MARK 11:24 ~

Jesus promised us that we would get those things that we ask for in prayer, if we believe that God will give them to us. If you pray and do not receive, accept that your request does not form part of God's plan for your life. But know too that He will always give you what is best for you.

Faith and trust go hand-in-hand: God's children should have faith in Him without harboring any doubt in their hearts that He will do what He has promised to do.

*God can do what He wills, when He wills, how He wills.*

~ JOHAN SMIT ~

Do you receive everything you ask for in prayer, or perhaps something even better? Give some examples.

# Success is possible

*Unless the Lord builds the house, its builders labor in vain. Unless the Lord watches over the city, the watchmen stand guard in vain. In vain you rise early and stay up late, toiling for food to eat – for he grants sleep to those he loves.*

~ Psalm 127:1-2 ~

The psalmist knew a secret that we should make our own: together with God, success is within our reach. If He helps you, you cannot help but be a winner!

But the opposite is also true. All your hard work and effort is worth nothing if God is not involved in what you do. He is the one who makes success possible and easy for you. Acknowledge Him in all your ways and He will put His miracle working power at your disposal.

*Most of the hindrances on your road to success are manmade. And all too often, you're the man who makes them.*

~ Frank Tyger ~

Do you have a personal recipe for success?
Write it down here.

# Be sensitive to the feelings of others

*My son, preserve sound judgment and discernment, do not let them out of your sight; they will be life for you, an ornament to grace your neck.*

~ Proverbs 3:21-22 ~

People who know how to treat people without rubbing them up the wrong way, will go far in life. Learn to speak and act appropriately, to take others into account, and the chances are they will do the same to you.

Pay particular attention to your words. Think carefully before you speak. Be sensitive to the feelings of others – don't say things that could cause permanent damage and that you will be sorry about later.

*If you can master the unspoken word,*
*you will be the master of the spoken word.*
~ Arabian Proverb ~

Think before you speak!

# Be patient

*Do nothing out of selfish ambition or vain conceit, but in humility consider others better than yourselves.*

~ Philippians 2:3 ~

It is innate in our human nature to always want to be first, and to see ourselves as more important than others. But that is not how God wants His children to behave. He expects us to be prepared to be the least important.

If other people's concerns carry more weight with you than your own, it will be easy to see when you do things wrong and so you will be willing to apologize and to be patient with others.

*It is a good thing to know that you are a Christian, but it is better to live so that others know that you are a Christian.*

~ Johan Smit ~

Try to be the first to say you're sorry when disagreements arise.

# Love

*"A new command I give you: Love one another. As I have loved you, so you must love one another."*

~ JOHN 13:34 ~

Our love for others should be a mirror image of Jesus' love for us. That is the essence of the new covenant that He gave to the world. And we will never be able to get it right without Him.

The love that God asks of you is not based on how good and nice the other person is, but it is to love them in spite of their faults and shortcomings. Ask God to give you this love through His Holy Spirit who lives in you.

*It is far easier to love humanity in general than it is to love each individual with whom you live and work.*

~ ERIC HOFFNER ~

Write down reasons why you should love those who don't deserve to be loved.

# Patience with others

*The Lord appeared to us in the past, saying: "I have loved you with an everlasting love; I have drawn you with loving-kindness.*

~ Jeremiah 31:3 ~

God had all the patience in the world with His rebellious people. And His love for them knew no bounds. No matter how disloyal they were to Him, even though they turned away from Him time after time to worship foreign gods, His love for them remained constant and He was always prepared to give them another chance.

The Lord wants you to have just as much patience with others as He has with you. He wants you to be as loyal to them as He is to you.

*Don't get thrown off course*
*when things go wrong around you.*
~ Johan Smit ~

How patient are you?

# You belong to God

*Even though I walk through the valley of the shadow of death, I will fear no evil, for you are with me; your rod and your staff, they comfort me.*

~ Psalm 23:4 ~

Children of God can remain calm in the midst of danger because they trust in Him. They know without a doubt that He is with them and that He promises to carry them through dangerous times.

Because you belong to God, you can face each day with strength and courage. Because He is with you, you need fear nothing. God will carry you and deliver you, even through the valley of death. In His hands you are always safe.

*To the extent that you learn to relax in the embrace of God's love, you will be set free from fear and will be able to love freely.*

~ Johan Smit ~

Does God's protection mean that you will never find yourself in dangerous situations?

# MAY

# He forgives

*In his distress he sought the favor of the Lord his God and humbled himself greatly before the God of his fathers. And when he prayed to him, the Lord was moved by his entreaty and listened to his plea; so he brought him back to Jerusalem and to his kingdom. Then Manasseh knew that the Lord is God.*

~ 2 Chronicles 33:12-13 ~

While King Manasseh was in exile, he confessed his sins before God and asked for His help. And God heard Manasseh's prayer. He allowed him to return to Jerusalem and to resume his reign of Judah.

God's mercy and forgiveness are indescribably great. He can and will forgive each one of your sins. If things go badly for you, confess your sins to God. He will forgive you and be gracious to you.

*Before we can be ready to receive the peace of forgiveness, we need to experience the remorse of repentance.*

~ Robert M. Herald ~

Write down the things for which you are asking God to forgive you.

# He will help you

*What, then, shall we say in response to this? If God is for us, who can be against us? No, in all these things we are more than conquerors through him who loved us.*

~ Romans 8:31, 37 ~

God is on His children's side. Therefore, there is nothing that can really be to their disadvantage or get them down. Even in hopeless situations they can be victors in the battle, because God fights for them and He is unconquerable.

God wants to offer you His help. Even when bad things happen to you, if God is on your side, nothing can be against you. In Him you are always more than a conqueror. He will help and support you in every situation.

*With God on your side, you will always be a winner.*

What does this mean in your life?

No matter what I experence or face – God will help me through it or over it!

# Faith means to keep believing

*Now faith is being sure of what we hope for and certain of what we do not see.*

~ Hebrews 11:1 ~

Faith means putting your doubts away for good. It means that you no longer insist on seeing visible signs of God's love and faithfulness, but that you will trust Him no matter how hard that may be. That you will keep hoping in Him even though you cannot see Him.

Faith is to keep believing, even when you cannot see, it is holding fast to God's promises even though you don't see one coming to pass. Faith makes the impossible possible.

*Talk faith. The world will be better off without your uttered ignorance and morbid doubt.*

~ Ella Wheeler Wilcox ~

Describe what faith means to you.

# God's almighty power

*Ignoring what they said, Jesus told the synagogue ruler, "Don't be afraid; just believe."*

~ Mark 5:36 ~

Jesus asked Jairus to keep believing even when someone came to tell him that his daughter was dead. It seems extremely unsympathetic to us, but Jesus had good reason to expect the impossible from Jairus – He Himself would ensure that Jairus's faith would not be disappointed. He raised his daughter from the dead.

It is hard to keep hoping when all hope seems gone, but if you can get it right, you will experience God's almighty power in your life.

*True faith is nothing more than doubt that has been consoled.*

~ Martin Luther ~

Write down the things that keep you from fully trusting God.

# Give the glory to God

*Each one should use whatever gift he has received to serve others, faithfully administering God's grace in its various forms.*

~ 1 PETER 4:10 ~

God made you so that you can do certain things well, so that you can excel in certain areas, not to garner money and honor for yourself. He wants you to know that these things are gifts of His grace to you and you should give Him the honor and glory through them and be prepared to serve others with those gifts.

You are a minister of God's grace. Live in such a way that other people can see Him in you, and will praise Him for the things you achieve.

*The number of gifts we have received is far less important than what we do with those we have received.*

Make a list of your gifts and talents and think about how you can use them to honor God.

# A flame of love

*We love because he first loved us.*

~ 1 John 4:19 ~

Love is a quality that no person receives as an innate attribute. God makes it possible for us to love Him and He makes it possible for you to love other people. Love comes from Him and He loved us while we were yet sinners and living far from Him.

God's love should ignite a flame of love in your heart – a flame that will warm those people around you.

*The Son shines not only on us but in us.*

~ John Muir ~

How do you live out God's love in your life?

# Complete trust

*Cast all your anxiety on him because he cares for you.*

~ 1 Peter 5:7 ~

People today are bowed down under the weight of countless anxieties. There are so many things that cause stress that about 90% of illnesses are attributed to excessive stress. And it is all so unnecessary. Become peaceful. Give your anxieties to God; He promises to care for you.

The definition of complete trust is bringing every one of your burdens to God, so that He can take over the care of them. Don't put it off any longer – do it right now!

*Carrying tomorrow's burden together with yesterday's today, causes even the strongest man to fall.*

~ Harvey Cushing ~

Make a list of the things that worry you, lay it before the Lord, and then tear it into little pieces.

# He is always there

*My help comes from the Lord, the Maker of heaven and earth. He will not let your foot slip – he who watches over you will not slumber.*

~ Psalm 121:2-3 ~

God is a Helper for His children. He is always ready to help us, to come quickly to our aid and to protect us. In just about every psalm this fact is asserted. Our Helper is almighty – not only is He the Creator of heaven and earth, He is also our personal God and always available for us. We can approach Him night and day.

You can take your problems to God any time of the night or day. He is always available and ready to help.

*Every grateful thought sent heavenwards is in itself a prayer.*

~ Glenn Clarke ~

You can be in contact with God 24 hours a day!

# Obedience to God

*I rejoice in following your statutes as one rejoices in great riches.*

~ Psalm 119:14 ~

The writer of Psalm 119 uncovered a great truth: people who live according to the dictates of God's Word are happy people. To do what God asks you to do is the sure way to be happy every day. If you make God happy, you will be happy!

True joy is to obey God and to honor Him. His law points you in the right direction and it brings greater joy than worldly riches and recognition.

*Joy in life does not come from the love of power, but from the power of love.*

~ M. Wells ~

What will you do today that will be pleasing to God?

# If you belong to God …

*Rejoice in the Lord always. I will say it again: Rejoice! Let your gentleness be evident to all. The Lord is near.*

~ Philippians 4:4-5 ~

Being happy is easy for the child of God. But even God's children struggle to be happy all the time. The closer we live to God, the easier it becomes to be filled with joy. We can be joyful because we are in His presence and we know that He cares for us.

If you belong to God, you can live with joy, even when things don't go well with you because you know that God has His arms around you all the time.

*How would we recognize joy if we did not have pain with which to compare it?*

~ Ena Murray ~

Write down five things that make you happy.

# Jesus paid on the cross

*In him we have redemption through his blood, the forgiveness of sins, in accordance with the riches of God's grace that he lavished on us with all wisdom and understanding.*

~ Ephesians 1:7-8 ~

When Jesus' blood flowed from the cross, it washed away the guilt of sin of those who believe in Him. God is willing to forgive our sins because Jesus reestablished peace between Him and us. We can never be grateful enough for this goodness of God.

Because Jesus paid the price of your sin on the cross, you can enjoy the riches of God's grace in your life each day, and live out of His abundance.

*The peace Christ gives us brings us peace with our fellowman.*

~ Johan Smit ~

Is there someone with whom you need to make peace?

# Closer to God

*But how is it to your credit if you receive a beating for doing wrong and endure it? But if you suffer for doing good and you endure it, this is commendable before God.*

~ 1 Peter 2:20 ~

When we deserve to be punished, it is easier and, in our eyes, more just, if we take our punishment like a man. But when we are punished unfairly, if we believe that we do not deserve to be punished, it is much more difficult to accept it.

You might sometimes suffer because of things that have not been your fault. God will give you the grace to accept such suffering. Undeserved punishment can in itself be an act of grace because it has the ability to bring you closer to God.

*The peace of God passes all understanding – even misunderstanding!*

~ Anonymous ~

Have you ever been unfairly treated? What happened?

# Deeds of love

*Bless those who curse you, pray for those who mistreat you. Do to others as you would have them do to you.*

~ Luke 6:28, 31 ~

God's love for you is indescribable – but because He loves you unconditionally, He expects you to love in the same way: that you will bless people who persecute you; that you will pray for those who seek to harm you. This sounds impossible to do, and so it is, but God makes it possible for you to love as He does.

God wants your love for Him to be translated into deeds of love – especially toward those people who least deserve it!

*The simplest good deed is better than the noblest good intention.*

~ Marthe Barmenthlo ~

Try to help someone today who least expects it.

# Give generously

*Each man should give what he has decided in his heart to give, not reluctantly or under compulsion, for God loves a cheerful giver.*

~ 2 Corinthians 9:7 ~

God does not have set regulations concerning the amounts we should give to Him – although a tenth was the expected amount in the Old Testament. He does not want us to feel under obligation to give some of our possessions and money to Him and others, but He wants us to give joyfully.

God loves people who are not stingy but who delight in giving to others. Ask Him to make you into a cheerful giver.

*The world asks, How much does he give?*
*Christ asks, Why does he give?*

~ John Mott ~

Are you a cheerful giver?

# God lives in you

*Splendor and majesty are before him;*
*strength and joy in his dwelling place.*
~ 1 Chronicles 16:27 ~

David wrote a delightful song of thanks for the Levites to sing before the ark of the Lord (see 1 Chr. 16:4-36). This song contrasts God's attributes with those of worthless people, and David comes to the conclusion that God is truly very great, that He is filled with glory and splendor, that strength and joy are found in His presence.

Joy is the legacy of God's children. Joy and peace fill the place that God inhabits continuously. And through His Spirit, God lives in you.

*The only way to guarantee*
*consistent joy is to live close to God.*

Why does God's presence make you glad?

# God cares for you

*Until now you have not asked for anything in my name.*
*Ask and you will receive, and your joy will be complete.*

~ John 16:24 ~

Shortly before Jesus was crucified, He explained to His disciples that believers have every reason to be glad. God ultimately changes the heartache of His children into gladness because He cares for us. If we come openly to God with our needs, He will hear our prayers and make our joy complete.

The awareness of God's love and care is an indisputable source of joy for all His children, including you.

*Joy is not a goal, but a consequence.*
~ Eleanor Roosevelt ~

Make a list of your most pressing needs.

# God guarantees a safe journey

*He stilled the storm to a whisper; the waves of the sea were hushed. They were glad when it grew calm, and he guided them to their desired haven.*

~ Psalm 107:29-30 ~

In Psalm 107 the psalmist gives a beautiful description of how God stills the storms in the lives of His children. He guarantees their safety on the stormy seas of life. They are assured that they will arrive safely at their destination, because He is with them.

When God is the captain of our ship, we can know for certain that He will guide us safely to the harbor where we long to be: heaven that He Himself has prepared for His children.

*Peace is not the absence of conflict from life, but the ability to cope with it.*

~ Unknown ~

What storms in your life has God stilled?

# God's flying lessons

*Like an eagle that stirs up its nest and hovers over its young, that spreads its wings to catch them and carries them on its pinions. The Lord alone led him; no foreign god was with him.*

~ Deuteronomy 32:11-12 ~

Eagles kick their young out of the nest when they think the babies are big enough to fly. This is not a very pleasant experience for the young eaglets, but it is necessary for them to test their wings. The parent eagles, however, hover near to make sure that the babies come to no harm.

God longs for you to reach spiritual maturity. That is why He sometimes pushes you out of the nest of your daily routine. When you encounter crises and problems, then God is teaching you how to fly!

*God gets His best soldiers out of the highlands of affliction.*

~ Charles Spurgeon ~

What have you learned through affliction?

# God forgives

*You will again have compassion on us; you will tread our sins underfoot and hurl all our iniquities into the depths of the sea.*

~ MICAH 7:19 ~

God is merciful. Not only does He not hold our sins against us, not only is He prepared to forgive us our sins, but He casts our sins into the sea of forgetfulness. He throws them into the deep blue sea, and never thinks of them again. And He asks us to do the same.

Forgiving is easier than forgetting. God is prepared to forget your sins, therefore you should be prepared to forgive people who sin against you in the same way. Are you nurturing a grudge against anyone? It's time to forget about it.

*Forgiveness is man's greatest need and his highest attainment.*

~ HORACE BUSHNELL ~

Be prepared not only to forgive others, but to forget their transgressions against you.

# Sinfulness

*For all have sinned and fall short of the glory of God, and are justified freely by his grace through the redemption that came by Christ Jesus.*

~ Romans 3:23-24 ~

Each person on earth is born a sinner. We do not naturally want to live close to God. But the good news is that He loves us so much that He would not leave us in our sinfulness. Through His grace He sets us free, because the death of Jesus on the cross paid the price for our sins.

Jesus offers reconciliation to you in place of the burden of your sin. You can never earn His grace. All you need to do to make this yours is to believe in Him.

*Grace is a single word that embraces all that God is for us in the Person of Jesus Christ.*

~ Lewis B. Smedes ~

What sins have you not yet confessed before God?

# *God wants to use you*

*Brothers, each man, as responsible to God, should remain in the situation God called him to.*

~ 1 Corinthians 7:24 ~

You might sometimes think that you would be able to serve God more effectively in a different place: on the mission field, or in a different town or city. But God has different ideas. He is the One who placed you, and your family, where you are, in your town, in your street, in your community.

God desires to use you to serve Him where you are right now. Begin to serve Him today, and don't keep yearning for different circumstances.

*I believe that doing good to others by serving them is the only justification for our existence, and the only source of perpetual joy.*

~ Gerhard Beukes ~

What can you do for God today, right where you are?

# He has given you all that you need

*"Bring the whole tithe into the storehouse, that there may be food in my house. Test me in this," says the Lord Almighty, "and see if I will not throw open the floodgates of heaven and pour out so much blessing that you will not have room enough for it."*

~ Malachi 3:10 ~

Malachi challenged the people of God to test God: if they were prepared to give Him the portion that He asked of them, He would undertake to care for them and bless them, far beyond what they could ever have imagined.

Are you prepared to accept the same challenge? God is always faithful to the promises in His Word. Give God the part of your income that rightly belongs to Him – and He will make sure that you have everything that you need – in abundance.

*Remember the charity that you have received,*
*forget that which you have shown others.*
~ Chilon ~

Are there still areas of your life
that you are holding back from God?

# Don't go to bed angry

*"In your anger do not sin": Do not let the sun go down while you are still angry.*

~ EPHESIANS 4:26 ~

It is very hard to fall asleep when you are extremely angry with someone else. Therefore, don't nurture your anger and hold it over till the next day. If you are unhappy, talk about it and clear the unpleasantness from the air, and then it will not be necessary to end your day with anger.

Restrain your temper. Don't ever go to bed angry. Make sure that all misunderstandings have been cleared up before the day is over.

*There is one way of clearing up all misunderstandings: the truth.*

~ FEDOROWICZ ~

Are you angry with someone? Who, and why?

# Listen to other people

*There is a time for everything, and a season for every activity under heaven: a time to tear and a time to mend, a time to be silent and a time to speak.*

~ ECCLESIASTES 3:1, 7 ~

It is unfortunate that so few people know this simple secret: there is a time to talk and a time to be silent. We usually can't wait to voice our own opinions, and so we listen impatiently to the opinions and ideas of others.

Communication involves both talking and listening. And communication is very important. Remember that there is a time when it is necessary for you to remain silent. Be prepared to listen to others' points of view before you air your own opinion.

*Be cautious with what you say. Words are powerful weapons that can cause much harm.*

~ PHIL BOSMANS ~

Are you a good listener?

# You are unique

*I praise you because I am fearfully and wonderfully made; your works are wonderful, I know that full well.*

~ Psalm 139:14 ~

Each person is a small miracle. The more science discovers about the human body, the more clearly we realize this. If you haven't yet been struck by the awesome way in which God made us, go and find an anatomy book in the library and read about your body. Never again will you feel unworthy. You are unique. God has made you in a wonderful way. In this world with its billions of people, there is only one you! You can be proud of the fact that God has made you so special.

*If you commit yourself to giving your all with the gifts and talents you have, nothing can stand in your way.*

~ Willem Cruywagen ~

What makes you unique, different from other people?

# Negative thoughts

*Above all else, guard your heart, for it is the wellspring of life.*

~ Proverbs 4:23 ~

Be careful of what you think. The way you think has a deep impact on your whole life. You are what you think! What your heart is filled with will ultimately determine the course of your life, says the writer of Proverbs. If you think negative thoughts all day long, your whole outlook on life will become negative and you will have a negative influence on others too. Teach yourself to think positive thoughts so that your life can be filled with light and joy.

*Our thoughts have a poweful influence over our bodies.*

~ André Maurois ~

Think positively!

# Give yourself to God

*Therefore, I urge you, brothers, in view of God's mercy, to offer your bodies as living sacrifices, holy and pleasing to God – this is your spiritual act of worship.*

~ Romans 12:1 ~

Believers should be prepared to surrender their whole life to God, to be living sacrifices that God will gladly receive. This is the essence of what serving God is all about.

If you want your spiritual life to be meaningful to yourself and others, you need to be prepared to give everything you have – including yourself – to God. Live so that you serve Him with every part of your life.

*A person who has discovered the secret of joyful service, has found the key that unlocks the joy of heaven.*

~ Corrie du Toit ~

In what ways are you serving God?

# Jesus triumphed over death

*And if Christ has not been raised, our preaching is useless and so is your faith.*

~ 1 Corinthians 15:14 ~

Paul declared that if Jesus did not rise from the dead, everything that he preached was meaningless and the faith of the Corinthians was groundless. Then they were still living in their sin, explained Paul in his letter.

But Jesus conquered death. He rose from the dead and lives forevermore so that you will be able to live with Him forever. That is why you need no longer live in sin.

*Death's but a path that must be trod*
*if man would ever pass to God.*

~ Thomas Parnell ~

What do you know about heaven?

# Jesus will come again

*"Men of Galilee," they said, "why do you stand here looking into the sky? This same Jesus, who has been taken from you into heaven, will come back in the same way you have seen him go into heaven."*

~ Acts 1:11 ~

Just after Jesus ascended to heaven, two men in white clothes told the group of astounded disciples who were staring up into the sky that Jesus would come again. He would return to His disciples in exactly the same way in which He went to His Father.

This promise is still valid for us today. Jesus will come again in glory – and all people will see Him. This will be a joyful event that you can anticipate with real hope.

*Teach me to recognize death as the opportunity to meet You face to face, and to learn to know You better.*

~ Teilhard de Chardin ~

Are you ready for Christ's return?

# No one knows

*He who testifies to these things says, "Yes, I am coming soon." Amen. Come, Lord Jesus.*

~ Revelation 22:20 ~

That Jesus will return is an undeniable fact, but when it will happen, no one knows, not even Jesus Himself. Only the Father knows when Jesus will return. And He is merciful. He is holding off the Second Coming of Christ until everyone has a chance to respond to His gift of grace.

You will see Jesus soon, if not at His Second Coming, then on the day you die. And not one of us knows when that will be. Live as if you expect Him everyday.

*We are sometimes so busy looking around us and in us, that we forget to look above us!*
~ Unknown ~

What would you do differently if you knew that Jesus was coming today?

# An instrument of God's peace

*Surely his salvation is near those who fear him, that his glory may dwell in our land.*

~ Psalm 85:9 ~

God desires everyone who believes in Him to have peace. But there is a condition to this promise of peace: they need to be prepared to serve Him and obey Him in all things He asks of them.

God offers His peace to you. If every Christian in the world is prepared to listen to God and to become an instrument of His peace, then His promise of peace will become a reality in our country.

*Make me an instrument of Your peace.*

~ Francis of Assisi ~

Do you experience the peace of God in your heart and life?

# JUNE

# Your Father is always near

*"I am the vine; you are the branches. If a man remains in me and I in him, he will bear much fruit; apart from me you can do nothing."*

~ JOHN 15:5 ~

Without the vine, the branches cannot even attempt to bear bunches of grapes. It is a physical impossibility. In the same way, the children of God cannot even try to bear fruit without God – it just cannot be done. But when we abide in Him, the fruit comes naturally.

You do not need to struggle on your own to get things right – your Father is always with you to help you. Without Him you can do nothing, but in His strength there is nothing that you cannot do.

*When I am weak, then I am strong.*

~ PAUL ~

Write out Galatians 5:22-23 in the space below.

# A purpose in every crisis

*And we know that in all things God works for the good of those who love him, who have been called according to his purpose. No, in all these things we are more than conquerors through him who loved us.*

~ ROMANS 8:28, 37 ~

It is unfortunately true that bad things often happen to good people. Things that are beyond our ability to explain rationally, and that are hard to reconcile with God's love. In such crises we can hold on to the truth that God causes all things to work together for our good.

Everything that happens to you is ultimately for your best because God has a purpose with each crisis that He allows to come your way. In His strength you can always be more than a conqueror.

*Sometimes God allows us to go through trials and tribulations so that we can examine ourselves thoroughly and rededicate our lives to Him.*

~ WILLIE JONKER ~

God will cause all things to work together for your good.

# Wisdom and insight

*They will still bear fruit in old age, they will stay fresh and green.*

~ PSALM 92:14 ~

People today are living longer than ever before. We are only just beginning to realize how much old people can contribute to society with the wisdom and insight and experience that they have gained over the years.

But getting older can also bring many negative things, and that is why we find it hard to comes to terms with growing old. When a person gets old, he is not less valuable to God. You can use the wisdom and insight that life has given you to increase your worth and value.

*To have reached old age and not to be thankful is, in my opinion, foolish.*

~ MANFRED HAUSMANN ~

Write down three things that growing older has taught you.

# Confess your own sin

*I confess my iniquity; I am troubled by my sin.*
~ PSALM 38:18 ~

The Bible tells us over and over again that it does not pay to try to hide our sins from God. It is of course impossible to do so, because He knows everything about us anyway. Ask Him to make you sensitive to the wrong things in your life that constantly plague you. Confess them one by one so that God can forgive you for them.

When relationships have gone wrong you need to confess your own sin before men and before God. Always be ready to be the first one to say that you're sorry.

*You only live once; but if you do it well, it is enough.*
~ UNKNOWN ~

Make a decision to be the first to say you're sorry.

# Believe that God knows best

*"For my thoughts are not your thoughts, neither are your ways my ways," declares the Lord. "As the heavens are higher than the earth, so are my ways higher than your ways and my thoughts than your thoughts."*

~ ISAIAH 55:8-9 ~

God thinks in ways that are completely different from the way we think. He also does things differently from us. And He always knows best, even if we cannot understand the way that He does things. All that we need to do is to keep believing that everything He does is the best for us.

God is incomparably great and wonderful. You will never be able to understand Him with your limited human understanding. And neither is it necessary for you to understand everything He does – simply believe that He knows best.

*The only light on the future is faith.*
~ THEODORE HOECKER ~

What God does is always for your best.

# Resist the devil

*Be self-controlled and alert. Your enemy the devil prowls around like a roaring lion looking for someone to devour. Resist him, standing firm in the faith, because you know that your brothers throughout the world are undergoing the same kind of sufferings.*

~ 1 PETER 5:8-9 ~

Even though some people think that there is no such thing as the devil, he is very much alive and he is stronger than you. But God gives you the weapons that you can use to overcome him. And Jesus conquered him on the cross.

You can do nothing to withstand the devil in your own strength. He is stronger than you, but in God's strength you can resist him and come out of the fray as the victor.

*God is always stronger than the devil; but remember that the devil is stronger than you.*

How will you overcome the devil in your life today?

# Forgive others

*"For if you forgive men when they sin against you, your heavenly Father will also forgive you."*

~ MATTHEW 6:14 ~

Jesus told His disciples that God would forgive them if they forgave others. If we understand the worth of God's forgiveness of us we will be prepared to forgive others. But it still remains difficult to keep forgiving someone who continuously makes us angry.

Love cannot be measured. Don't try to count how many times you have forgiven someone. Be prepared to forgive them every time, as God does with you.

*When we experience forgiveness, it will affect our relationships with those closest to us.*

~ HELMUT THIELICKE ~

Do you still count how many times you have forgiven others?

# Be careful what you say

*I said, "I will watch my ways and keep my tongue from sin; I will put a muzzle on my mouth as long as the wicked are in my presence."*

~ PSALM 39:1 ~

Many of us harm others by the things that we thoughtlessly say about them. Before you say something about someone else, consider that you can never take back the words that you speak. What's been said has been said.

Our sharp words can wound another person. Children of the Lord must try to set a guard before their mouths at all times. Think very carefully before you blurt something out that you will later regret.

*The tongue has the power of life and death,*
*and those who love it will eat its fruit.*
PROVERBS 18:21

Do you manage to set a guard before your mouth, to think before you speak?

# You should be a light-bearer

*"You are the light of the world. A city on a hill cannot be hidden. In the same way, let your light shine before men, that they may see your good deeds and praise your Father in heaven."*

~ MATTHEW 5:14, 16 ~

Jesus proclaimed that He is the light of the world. But His children are also lights – lights that shine before other people so that they can see the good things we do and so glorify our heavenly Father.

As a planet reflects the light of the sun, God wants us to bear His light in this world. When people look at you they should see Jesus in the things that you do and say.

*Do not shut yourself off from the world; give yourself to it.*

~ WALTER RINDER ~

What are you doing to reflect the light of God around you?

# The right road

*I will instruct you and teach you in the way you should go; I will counsel you and watch over you.*

~ PSALM 32:8 ~

God offers to guide His children: He wants to teach them and show them the right road. He wants to counsel us when we need advice, and He watches over us all the time.

God loves you so much that He knows exactly where you are at the moment, and what you are busy doing. You can always get help and counsel from Him. He watches over you and directs you along the path that you should follow.

*God gives people wisdom like He gave the earth gold: His treasury is not the mint but the mine.*

~ UNKNOWN ~

Ask God to reveal the path He has set for you through life.

# The best response to God

*Give thanks to the Lord, for he is good; his love endures forever.*

~ PSALM 107:1 ~

God's children experience His goodness and mercy every day. When you pause and consider God's overwhelming love and mercy for you, you will not be able to stop yourself from singing praises to Him.

The best response that you can give God for His goodness to you is to sing a song of praise to Him. Don't ever stop praising Him!

*Praise to God is an integral part of a joyful heart.*

Write a personal song of praise to God.

# Faith is essential

*"Have faith in God," Jesus answered. "I tell you the truth, if anyone says to this mountain, 'Go, throw yourself into the sea,' and does not doubt in his heart but believes that what he says will happen, it will be done for him."*

~ Mark 11:22-23 ~

Faith can perform wonders. But faith is not to be used to try to manipulate God for the things we selfishly desire. When we pray we must believe that God will give us those things that we ask of Him, as long as they are in His will.

Faith should be the Christian's steering wheel, and not the spare wheel. It is an essential part of your life that should not just be taken out in emergencies.

*Faith is not a sense, nor sight, nor reason, but taking God at His Word.*

Remember that faith is not the spare wheel in your life.

# A God of miracles

*Then Jesus said, "Did I not tell you that if you believed, you would see the glory of God?"*

~ JOHN 11:40 ~

The sisters of Lazarus, and all the others who were present, were speechless when Jesus raised Lazarus back to life from the dead. It seemed completely impossible. But God is almighty. He can do the impossible. And He is still able to perform miracles.

God's words are true for us too. If we believe, we will see the demonstration of His power. If you believe, you will discover that God is a God of miracles. Nothing is impossible for Him.

*He who prays without confidence cannot hope that his prayers will be granted.*

~ FÉNELON ~

What miracles have you experienced in your life?

# Christians always win

*I can do everything through him who gives me strength.*
~ Philippians 4:13 ~

Paul was able to achieve wonderful things because God was his source of strength. And God's strength is just as available to us as it was to Paul. We too can draw on His strength when we encounter crises in our lives. Over and over we find that we can do all things because God gives us His strength. God makes His miracle-working power available to all His children.

If you are facing difficult situations, you can be on the winning side if you know where your strength comes from. There is nothing that you and God cannot achieve together.

*What cannot be achieved through expertise and experience can only be achieved through faith.*
~ W. A. Hofmeyr ~

Accept God's miracle working power in your life today.

# Show your love

*Dear children, let us not love with words or tongue but with actions and in truth.*

~ 1 John 3:18 ~

Words do not mean much unless you are prepared to put action to your promises. This is also true of our love for God, says John. We need to show our love by the things that we do, and these acts of love need to be sincere, too.

If you realize the extent of God's love for you, and how much it cost Him to bring His love to you, you will be compelled to show your love for Him by your loving actions.

*Love opens our hearts to give without measure.*

~ Piet Naudé ~

Do something today that will once again show your love for God.

# God will never let you down

*I will lie down and sleep in peace, for you alone, O Lord, make me dwell in safety.*

~ Psalm 4:8 ~

Christians have a deep sense of peace that other people find hard to understand. Because we know that God loves us, we also know that God promises to protect us, that He will never disappoint us, and that we are assured of His presence each day. Therefore, we do not need to lie awake at night worrying.

You can live each day with joy and sleep peacefully each night because the One you trust will never let you down.

*When despair says, "There is a cloud hiding the sun," faith says, "Behind every cloud, the sun is shining!"*

~ F. V. Vledder ~

What are you trusting God for?

# God is there for His children

*For he wounds, but he also binds up; he injures, but his hands also heal. From six calamities he will rescue you; in seven no harm will befall you.*

~ Job 5:18-19 ~

Job knew in his heart that he would not always be able to protect his children from disasters and trouble. He literally lost everything, except his faith in the God who was testing him. Eliphas, his friend, assured him that God would bind up his wounds and would ultimately deliver him.

Sometimes God allows disasters to strike His children but He is always there to help them when they ask Him for His help.

*The brightest crowns that are worn in heaven*
*have been tried, and smelted, and polished, and*
*glorified through the furnace of tribulation.*
~ E. H. Chapin ~

What trials in your life are you
able to look back on with gratitude?

# Grace is a free gift

*It does not, therefore, depend on man's desire or effort, but on God's mercy.*

~ Romans 9:16 ~

God's decision to adopt people as His children is not dependent on anything that we do or don't do. He calls people to Himself because of His grace. And He owes us nothing. He shows mercy to those whom He chooses.

You cannot do anything that will influence Him in His decision. If you accept His offer of mercy, you should never stop thanking Him for His grace toward you.

*Grace is not only a gift, but carries with it a responsibility.*

What meaning does God's grace have for you personally?

# Sincere sympathy

*Then Job replied: "Listen carefully to my words; let this be the consolation you give me."*

~ JOB 21:1-2 ~

Job was deeply appreciative of the sympathy his three friends showed him by sitting silently with him for a whole week while he was suffering his traumatic losses. But when they began to talk to him, their words upset him horribly.

Sometimes we do not know what to say to someone who is going through difficult times. A hug and sincere sympathy for someone who is facing problems is far better comfort than a string of meaningless words.

*Don't use your big mouth to belittle someone else.*

~ PHIL BOSMANS ~

Show people you care, without using any words!

# No one knows the future

*To them God has chosen to make known among the Gentiles the glorious riches of this mystery, which is Christ in you, the hope of glory.*

~ Colossians 1:27 ~

In the New Testament, God reveals the secret that He had hinted at in the Old Testament: Jesus makes heaven accessible to all of us, even those people who do not belong to God's special nation. If you believe in Him, He comes to live in you. He is your hope for the future.

Not one of us knows just what the future holds in store but if we know Jesus we know that He will be present in our future. He is our only hope for reaching the heaven that we long for.

*God's children do not know what their future holds, but they know who holds the future.*

What are your dreams for the future?

# God sets you free

*But now that you have been set free from sin and have become slaves to God, the benefit you reap leads to holiness, and the result is eternal life.*

~ ROMANS 6:22 ~

To live in sin is a dead end street. But God sets us free from our sins and takes us into His service. He guarantees that we will have eternal life. But the responsibility to be the kind of person that God wants us to be lies with us.

If God has set you free from your sins, you should use your new freedom to serve Him and to live a holy life. Then you will be assured of eternal life.

*There is no true holiness without humility.*

~ THOMAS FULLER ~

What things in your life do you need to sacrifice in order to be holy?

# Spiritual growth

*You do not have, because you do not ask God. Come near to God and he will come near to you. Wash your hands, you sinners, and purify your hearts, you double-minded.*

~ JAMES 4:2, 8 ~

Although many people pray, they do not often receive answers to their prayers, because they live far from God. People who love God and live close to Him find that God draws near to them and He gives them the things that they ask for.

Prayer is the thermometer that measures the spiritual growth and strength of Christians. What does your prayer life look like? If you stay close to God He will hear your prayers and help you become spiritually stronger day by day.

*The purpose of prayer is not to inform God of our needs, but to invite Him to show us where He has need of us.*

~ CARDINAL BAUMANN ~

Rate your prayer life on a scale of 1-10. What can you do to improve your score?

# He controls your life

*But just as he who called you is holy, so be holy in all you do.*

~ 1 PETER 1:15 ~

The same God who calls us to be His children is holy and without sin. And He expects us to have nothing to do with sin. Ask Him to show you the things in your life that are sinful and to help you to get rid of them once and for all, so that you can become more like Jesus.

If you allow the Holy Spirit to take control of your life, God can turn a sinful human being into a saint.

*I surrender all. All to Thee my*
*blessed savior, I surrender all.*

~ HYMN ~

Are you ready and willing to surrender every aspect of your life to the Holy Spirit?

# Prayer is a conversation

*"Ask and it will be given to you; seek and you will find; knock and the door will be opened to you."*

~ Matthew 7:7 ~

God's children should never grow tired of praying. What we ask for in prayer, God promises to do. We never walk away from God empty handed. That is why we feel so much better when we have laid our desires at the feet of God.

Prayer is a conversation between two people who love each other. When you pray, God gives you what you ask for, providing that it is within His will.

*Pray in the Holy Spirit.*
~ Jude 20 ~

Are your conversations with God simply repetitions of what you have said previously?

# God knows your needs

*"For your Father knows what you need before you ask him."*
~ Matthew 6:8 ~

It is not necessary to pray long-winded prayers in which you list each of your requests to God. This was what Jesus told His disciples when they asked Him to teach them to pray. God knows us so well that He already knows exactly what our needs are long before we put them into words. God knows you personally and intimately and He knows each one of your needs. He knows exactly what you need before you ask Him.

*Prayer does not have to follow a set pattern or make use of elegant words. Prayer is a lifestyle.*
~ Ferdinand Deist ~

What would you like to ask God today?

# God gives you strength

*Three times I pleaded with the Lord to take it away from me. But he said to me, "My grace is sufficient for you, for my power is made perfect in weakness." Therefore I will boast all the more gladly about my weaknesses, so that Christ's power may rest on me.*

~ 2 CORINTHIANS 12:8-9 ~

Paul prayed earnestly that God would remove the thorn that hindered him, but God did not answer his prayer. He wanted Paul to learn that His power works most effectively when His children are weak. His grace is sufficient for us.

Sometimes God does not change your circumstances, but He always gives you the strength to work through your situation in a positive way. And when you are weak, His strength is at its most effective.

*Faith does not mean believing without evidence, but to believe without reservation.*

~ ELTON TRUEBLOOD ~

Are you able to believe without reservation?

# Learn to pray by praying

*One day Jesus was praying in a certain place. When he finished, one of his disciples said to him, "Lord, teach us to pray, just as John taught his disciples."*

~ LUKE 11:1 ~

The disciples of Jesus saw how much joy and strength He derived from the fellowship of prayer He enjoyed with the Father. That is why they asked Him to teach them to pray.

Perhaps you have wished that Jesus could teach you to pray. All that you need to do if you desire to talk to God is simply to talk to Him. Tell God what is in your heart. Just as we learned to write by practicing writing, we learn to pray by praying.

*When prayer becomes a way of life, a continuous awareness of the presence of God, then life itself becomes a liturgy, an offering of worship to the Lord.*

~ FERDINAND DEIST ~

Keep a record of your prayers for seven days.

# A song of praise

*Let everything that has breath praise the Lord. Praise the Lord.*
~ Psalm 150:6 ~

The whole of Psalm 150 is an exuberant song of praise to God. The psalmist invites everyone to join him in his song of praise and to praise God for who He is. God deserves to be praised with every kind of musical instrument imaginable by everyone who has breath.

When you are feeling depressed and discouraged, sing a song of praise to God. Praise Him in every possible way. You will find that your heaviness will dissipate like the mist before the sun.

*Praise the Lord, O my soul; all my inmost being, praise his holy name.*
~ Psalm 103:1 ~

Each day this week, read one of the psalms of praise as a prayer to God.

# His perfect will

*"Not everyone who says to me, 'Lord, Lord,' will enter the kingdom of heaven, but only he who does the will of my Father who is in heaven."*

~ MATTHEW 7:21 ~

These words of Jesus leave us with an uneasy feeling: only those people who do what He says will find a place in His new kingdom. Getting to heaven requires more from you than just saying the right words. You also need to be prepared to be obedient to God.

Are you prepared to submit your own desires to God's will? Only when His perfect will rules in your life will you be completely happy.

*When you begin to do God's will in the obvious things, you will have fewer questions about the things that are not as clear.*

~ JOHAN SMIT ~

Pray that God's will be done in your life.

# Seek God's kingdom first

*"But seek first his kingdom and his righteousness, and all these things will be given to you as well."*
~ MATTHEW 6:33 ~

Do the things that are important to God, be obedient to His will, ensure that His Kingdom grows, and He will take care of all the other things in your life. This is what Jesus promises in the Sermon on the Mount. God provides for each one of His children's needs. We do not need to worry about tomorrow because He will care for us in the future as well.

If you are prepared to put God's Kingdom first He will meet each one of your needs.

*Obedience to God is the most infallible evidence of sincere and supreme love to him.*
~ NATHANAEL EMMONS ~

What choices will you make to show that you put God's Kingdom first in your life?

# JULY

# God is with you all day

*Pray continually.*

~ 1 Thessalonians 5:17 ~

It is a good idea to make an appointment in your diary every day to spend time with God. But you can also speak to God at any time during the day – not just during the time set aside for your devotions. God is always ready to listen to what you have to say.

Try to pray at different and unusual moments during the day: when you are waiting for the lights to change, when you are in a supermarket queue, while you're preparing supper, at the post office, at work ... in this way you will be aware that God is with you all through the day.

*To be in God's thoughts means that we are also in His hands.*

~ Johan Smit ~

Write down two different and unusual places where you can talk to God.

# A way of life

*But when you pray, go into your room, close the door and pray to your Father, who is unseen. Then your Father, who sees what is done in secret, will reward you.*

~ MATTHEW 6:6 ~

Ferdinand Deist, in his book on prayer, says that prayer is a way of life. God wants continuous and faithful communication with Him to be an integral part of His children's lives. Can you imagine what your life would be like if you never talked to God?

Set aside time each day to be alone with God. The busier your day is, the more you need your quiet time. Talk to God about everything in your life. In this way prayer will become a way of life for you.

*Powerful contact with God leads*
*to powerful contact with people.*
~ AN UNKNOWN CHRISTIAN ~

Make a prayer list for each day of the week.

# God knows you

*Your eyes saw my unformed body. All the days ordained for me were written in your book before one of them came to be.*

~ PSALM 139:16 ~

The psalmist is awed by the fact that God knows him so well, that He knew him even before he was born, that God had already then planned each day of his life.

God knows you just as thoroughly. He knew you before you were born, too. He knows exactly what each day of your life will be like. You can hide nothing from Him. And simply because God knows you so well, you can trust Him completely.

*For a man's ways are in full view of the Lord, and he examines all his paths.*

~ PROVERBS 5:21 ~

What affect does it have in your life when you think that you can hide nothing from God?

# God gives abundantly

*I am the Lord your God, who brought you up out of Egypt. Open wide your mouth and I will fill it.*

~ Psalm 81:10 ~

God reassures His people over and over again that He will care for them because He is their God. He promises not only to give them the things that they need, but also that He will give far more than what is needed. And He honors His word.

If you belong to God, He makes this promise to you, too. God is with you every day and He will take good care of you. He never does things in half-measures; He gives abundantly.

*Without God we cannot. Without us, God will not.*

~ Augustine ~

Praise God for His abundant provisions.

# The good news of God's love

*I am obligated both to Greeks and non-Greeks, both to the wise and the foolish. That is why I am so eager to preach the gospel also to you who are at Rome.*

~ ROMANS 1:14-15 ~

The love of God compelled Paul to tell as many people as he could the good news of Jesus. He longed to minister the gospel to people in Rome so that those who had never before heard about Jesus could also be saved.

The grace of God makes you into a debtor: you owe people around you the good news of God's love. You should never be ashamed to witness for Him.

*The power of the Spirit makes you a powerful witness.*

To whom do you owe the message of God's love?

# The sincerity of your love

*I am not commanding you, but I want to test the sincerity of your love by comparing it with the earnestness of others.*

~ 2 Corinthians 8:8 ~

The way you treat less advantaged people shows whether your love for the Lord is genuine or mere lip service, so Paul tells the Corinthians. He went on to encourage them to do good deeds by telling them how committed other Christians are to supporting and assisting the disadvantaged.

The sincerity of your love for the Lord is still measured by what you are prepared to offer for His kingdom. What do you do for people who have less than you do?

*It is astonishing how little one feels poverty when one loves.*

~ John Bulwer ~

What principles of love do you bring to God's kingdom?

# Live for Jesus

*In the same way, count yourselves dead*
*to sin but alive to God in Christ Jesus.*

~ Romans 6:11 ~

Sin no longer has a hold on God's children. The sinful nature with which they were born no longer holds sway in their lives. They are dead to sin. They should now live for God because they have been made one with Christ.

To be holy means that once you are born again you reckon yourself as dead to sin and alive to Jesus. Are you prepared to live for Jesus?

*We must understand that the Spirit of God is called*
*the Holy Spirit because He purposefully and*
*expressly desires to share God's holiness with us.*

~ Andrew Murray ~

In what specific ways do you
want to begin to live for Jesus?

# Live in holiness

*Do not offer the parts of your body to sin, as instruments of wickedness, but rather offer yourselves to God, as those who have been brought from death to life; and offer the parts of your body to him as instruments of righteousness. For sin shall not be your master, because you are not under law, but under grace.*

~ ROMANS 6:13-14 ~

Christians should be careful never to yield any part of their body to sin. They should be completely committed to God. Every part of their lives should be dedicated to God and to doing the things that He asks them, in His Word, to do.

If you are willing to offer every part of your body to the service of God then He, through the Holy Spirit who lives in you, will help you to live a holy life.

*Being filled with the Spirit is surrendering to the Spirit completely.*

~ WILLIE JONKER ~

What does holiness mean to you?

# Trust God

*As the Scripture says, "Anyone who trusts in him will never be put to shame."*

~ ROMANS 10:11 ~

When you work with people, you very quickly discover that few people are really trustworthy. People are not perfect, and so it is almost inevitable that at one time or another someone will let you down. The trust that you have placed in them will be broken.

But God is different. If you believe in God and trust Him you can be sure of one thing: He will never disappoint you.

*My faith is more important than my status.*

~ JÖRG ZINK ~

Live so that others can trust you completely.

# Eternal life

*Jesus said to her, "I am the resurrection and the life. He who believes in me will live, even though he dies; and whoever lives and believes in me will never die. Do you believe this?"*

~ JOHN 11:25-26 ~

When Martha asked Jesus why He had not prevented her brother from dying, He explained that He is the resurrection and the life: the one who raises people from the dead and gives them a life that never ends.

Everyone who believes in Jesus is assured of eternal life. When Jesus died on the cross He made it possible for you to live forever. That is why you can already have the assurance that you have eternal life.

*We all need to prepare for the future, because we will spend the rest of our lives there.*
~ CHARLES KETTERING ~

Are you certain that you have eternal life?

# Faith always produces results

*He replied, "If you have faith as small as a mustard seed, you can say to this mulberry tree, 'Be uprooted and planted in the sea,' and it will obey you."*

~ Luke 17:6 ~

All that is needed to make the impossible possible is faith as small as a mustard seed, the smallest of all seeds, so said Jesus to His disciples.

Even if your faith is very small, God is ready to listen to you. God responds to the requests His children make. Faith is calling out to God. Faith will not be silenced, and faith always produces results.

*The proverb says: To see is to believe, but Biblical faith works differently. It says: Not to see is to believe.*

~ Johan Smit ~

Write a definition of faith in the space below.

# God promises you His joy

*Make us glad for as many days as you have afflicted us, for as many years as we have seen trouble.*

~ Psalm 90:15 ~

The psalmist prays that God will give Him as many days of joy as the days of heaviness that he has endured. God's children need never live without hope, no matter how bad things seem. They are assured of a happy ending, of eternity in heaven together with God. Your trials and tribulations on earth endure only for a short while. And then the difficult times will end and God promises that you will have joy forevermore.

*Grief and pain are but the soil from which springs the lovely plant – unselfishness.*

~ Helen Keller ~

What comfort do you have when you go through hard times?

# You are the church of God

*Now you are the body of Christ, and each one of you is a part of it.*
~ 1 CORINTHIANS 12:27 ~

Not one of us is satisfied with every single decision that is made within our congregations. We find it easy to criticize and might even decide not to go to church any more. But who is actually the church? Not the congregation nor the building. The church of God is made up of individuals – just like you.

Next time you feel like criticizing your church or congregation remember that you are part of the community of God, the church of God upon this earth. Therefore, if you really want to see things change, start with yourself.

*It is easier to fight for one's*
*principles than to live according to them.*
~ ALFRED ADLER ~

How do you contribute to your congregation?

# Use your gifts

*Now to each one the manifestation of the Spirit is given for the common good. All these are the work of one and the same Spirit, and he gives them to each one, just as he determines.*

~ 1 Corinthians 12:7, 11 ~

The Holy Spirit works in a unique way in each of God's children. God has given each one of us gifts that we can use to serve our fellowman. But sadly we are so inclined to compare our gifts with what others can do that we end up neglecting our own.

Each of us has different kinds of gifts, and giftings in different degrees. But God has given each one of us specific gifts with which we can glorify Him and that should be used in His service. Use the gifts He has given you to honor Him.

*Your talents are God's gift to you.*
*What you do with them is your gift to Him.*
~ Unknown ~

Do you know what your gifts are?

# Follow Jesus

*Then he called the crowd to him along with his disciples and said: "If anyone would come after me, he must deny himself and take up his cross and follow me."*

~ Mark 8:34 ~

Jesus is never satisfied with half measures. If you follow Him you must be prepared to take second place, to leave everything behind you, to give your whole life to Him, even to endure hard times and yet serve Him.

It is worthwhile to forsake all things and follow Jesus. The joy that disciples experience is far greater than the pain of any demands that might be made on you.

*If we would do much for God, we should ask much from Him.*

~ The Unknown Christian ~

What does it mean to you to be a disciple of Jesus?

# Your possessions

*Jesus looked at him and loved him. "One thing you lack," he said. "Go, sell everything you have and give to the poor, and you will have treasure in heaven. Then come, follow me." At this the man's face fell. He went away sad, because he had great wealth.*

~ MARK 10:21-22 ~

It might seem to you that Jesus set excessively high expectations on the rich young man. How many of us would really be prepared to sell all we have, give the proceeds to the poor in order to "lay up treasures in heaven?"

Jesus does not expect you to get rid of all your assets. When your possessions become a higher priority in your life than your relationship with God, you should hear a warning bell begin to ring in your heart.

*It is good to have money and possessions, but is also good to make sure, from time to time, that you do not lose the things that money cannot buy.*
~ G. H. LORRIMER ~

Which of your possessions is dearest to you?

# He chose you

*For he chose us in him before the creation of the world to be holy and blameless in his sight.*

~ EPHESIANS 1:4 ~

People have different opinions on the concept of predestination. Some think that it is unfair that there are many people who will never be given the chance to make a decision for God. But before the creation of the world God had decided who His children would be.

You do not need to tire yourself out trying to understand predestination. God decides in His mercy who His children will be. If you hear His voice and respond to it, you will know that He has chosen you.

*Jesus bridged the chasm between heaven and earth when He died on the cross.*

Have you responded to God's voice? Thank Him for chosing you before the world was created.

# When we meet God

*"God did this so that men would seek him and perhaps reach out for him and find him, though he is not far from each one of us. 'For in him we live and move and have our being.' As some of your own poets have said, 'We are his offspring.'"*

~ Acts 17:27-28 ~

We all long for peace. One of the early church fathers, Augustine, wrote a prayer that has become very famous: "Thou hast made us for Thyself, O Lord; and our heart is restless until it rests in Thee."

God created people with a desire to seek Him. There is a longing in each one of us that can only be stilled when we meet God. Don't stop looking until you find God.

*Nothing is more important in life than your relationship with God.*

Have you had an encounter with God?

# Eyes of love

*My brothers, as believers in our glorious Lord Jesus Christ, don't show favoritism.*

~ James 2:1 ~

When we talk about other people, we tend to criticize or judge them according to our limited understanding of their lives and circumstances: what they look like, where they live, what work they do and what kind of car they drive. We seem to think that rich and popular people are much more important than ordinary, average people.

God never looks at people in terms of dollars and cents, but through eyes of love. Guard against judging people on outward appearances. Rather look at them through the eyes of God's love.

*God sees you, whoever you are, as you are ... He calls you by name, He sees you and He understands you because He created you.*

~ Jörg Zink ~

Through which glasses do you look at others?

# In God's Service

*Whatever your hand finds to do, do it with all your might, for in the grave, where you are going, there is neither working nor planning nor knowledge nor wisdom.*

~ ECCLESIASTES 9:10 ~

No one knows how long his life will be. That is why we should diligently put our hand to the tasks that lie before us.

Do not be lazy. Be prepared to do your part in the kingdom of God. If you are prepared to give your strength, talents and time in God's service you will find that your life here on earth will be good preparation for your life in heaven.

*You will learn to respect yourself*
*when you learn to help other people.*

~ B. W. WOODS ~

What will you do to extend God's Kingdom?

# Be available for others

*And he has given us this command: Whoever loves God must also love his brother. Everyone who believes that Jesus is the Christ is born of God, and everyone who loves the father loves his child as well.*

~ 1 John 4:21; 5:1 ~

If we love God, we should also love other people. God expects this of His children: each one who loves Him should love his fellow believers too. John says that if you do not love people whom you can see, then you do not love God whom you cannot see.

God showed how much He loves you by letting His Son die in your place. You should show your love for Him by loving other people and being available to help them.

*Love does not simply make us resourceful in the offering of help, it first makes us resourceful in the awareness of need.*

~ Helmut Thielicke ~

Do you make yourself available for those in need?

# Be sensitive to the needs of others

*Our desire is not that others might be relieved while you are hard pressed, but that there might be equality. At the present time your plenty will supply what they need, so that in turn their plenty will supply what you need. Then there will be equality.*

~ 2 CORINTHIANS 8:13-14 ~

Paul writes to the Corinthians that he does not expect them to give so much to others that they will themselves lack what they need. But those people who have more than enough should be prepared to help those who do not have enough.

There are many people around you who go to sleep hungry at night. What are you doing to help them? We should all be prepared to take note of the needs of people around us and to help as far as we are able.

*Before love moves our hands, it opens our eyes.*

~ HELMUT THIELICKE ~

What needs are you aware of around you?

# The Lord requires your willingness

*For it is God who works in you to will*
*and to act according to his good purpose.*
~ PHILIPPIANS 2:13 ~

We are not able to achieve anything in our own strength – especially regarding the work we do in God's kingdom. But God promises to equip us and make us willing to do the things that He requires of us and so fulfill His purpose. All we need to do is report for duty.

The Lord does not expect you to be highly competent before He will use you in His service – all that He wants from you is your willingness. He will do the rest.

*A life lived in the service of others is a life well-lived.*
~ ADRIO KÖNIG ~

Are you prepared to be used by God?

# The sacrifice of your faith

*But even if I am being poured out like a drink offering on the sacrifice and service coming from your faith, I am glad and rejoice with all of you.*

~ Philippians 2:17 ~

In Old Testament times the priests brought sacrifices of animals to God so that He would forgive His people. Sacrifices are never easy – the animal had to be slaughtered, blood had to flow before God would accept the sacrifices.

Jesus' blood flowed for you when He died on the cross. And your walk of faith is not always a picnic. It sometimes requires sacrifices from you. And the sacrifices of your faith are seen in a life committed to serving God.

*Our sacrifice in service of others makes us sympathetic to the sufferings of others.*

~ Daniël Louw ~

What does Christ's sacrifice on the cross mean for you personally?

# Your salvation

*I am not ashamed of the gospel, because it is the power of God for the salvation of everyone who believes: first for the Jew, then for the Gentile.*

~ Romans 1:16 ~

Paul was never embarrassed to share the good news about Jesus with other people. It was important to him that every person should hear the message of salvation. He realized the power of God that brings about salvation for everyone who believes in His name, is in the gospel message.

Believing in Jesus is still the key that unlocks the door to your salvation. And faith means that you do not need to contribute anything to your redemption. All you need to do is accept the gift of grace God offers to you.

*Faith is to believe, on the Word of God, what we do not see, and its reward is to see and enjoy what we believe.*

~ Augustine ~

Have you ever reached out to God and received the gift of faith?

# Jesus was a person like you

*For we do not have a high priest who is unable to sympathize with our weaknesses, but we have one who has been tempted in every way, just as we are – yet was without sin.*

~ Hebrews 4:15 ~

When God sent His Son into the world, He was both truly God and truly man. Jesus was completely without sin, yet He was also tempted just as we are. But He never succumbed to temptation.

Because Jesus was a person just like us, He knows exactly what we go through when we face temptations. He can sympathize with your human weaknesses. And He promises to help you and to strengthen you when temptations come your way.

*It is not enough to serve Jesus, we must become like Him.*

~ Derek Copley ~

What does it mean to you that Jesus became human, just as you are?

# Pure thoughts

*Finally, brothers, whatever is true, whatever is noble, whatever is right, whatever is pure, whatever is lovely, whatever is admirable – if anything is excellent or praiseworthy – think about such things.*

~ PHILIPPIANS 4:8 ~

Paul says that the Philippians should make sure that their thoughts reflect the things that are important to God. Their thoughts should focus on everything that is good and perfect rather than wasting time thinking about sinful and worthless things.

The things that you think about determine how you look at life. That is why you should make an effort to keep your thoughts pure. Think only of those things that are beautiful and worthwhile and your life will reflect the positive thoughts that you think.

*All of our dignity consists in thought. Let us endeavor then to think well; this is the principle of morality.*

~ BLAISE PASCAL ~

Set your thoughts on "things above."

# God is always right

*You have made known to me the path of life; you will fill me with joy in your presence, with eternal pleasures at your right hand.*

~ Psalm 16:11 ~

The psalmist knows the truth that the secret of true joy is found only in God, and that He always gives the very best to His children. Even so, we still go through hard times in our lives. In these times we can still depend on God's support.

During the difficult times in our lives, we simply need to hold God's hand more tightly. What He does is always right. What He brings into your life is always good. What He has planned for your life is always the best for you.

*God does not always give us an answer*
*to the why of suffering. But He does promise*
*that He will be with us in every crisis.*

~ J. E. de Vries ~

Where do you find comfort in times of trouble?

# Control your thoughts

*We take captive every thought to make it obedient to Christ.*

~ 2 Corinthians 10:5 ~

The secret of controlling negative thoughts is to ask yourself if God would be pleased with the things that you are thinking. Ask Him to purify your thoughts and help you to reject all negative and wrong thoughts.

Next time you begin to think negative thoughts, thoughts that are not appropriate for a Christian, you need to consciously take those thoughts captive. You can control your thought life with God's help, and be obedient to God.

*Keep your thoughts right – for as you think, so you are. Thoughts are things, therefore think only things that will make the world better and you unashamed.*

~ Henry Buckley ~

Ask God to help you focus your thoughts on Him.

# Joy in hard times

*Though the fig tree does not bud and there are no grapes on the vines ... yet will I rejoice in the Lord, I will be joyful in God my Savior.*

~ Habakkuk 3:17-18 ~

Christians have a unique characteristic – they can praise God even when they are in the middle of trials and tribulations because they know that He is fully in control.

Habakkuk could continue to rejoice in spite of the fact that everything was going wrong in his life. When you have absolute trust in God you, too, will be able to keep rejoicing. Even though you might not understand why God sometimes allows such difficult things in your life.

*Faith can help you change direction, light the path before you, get rid of any distress; it changes heartache into joy, tension into peace ... hell into heaven.*

~ F. L. Holmes ~

Write down some of the highlights of your life.

# God's guidelines

*Do not be overcome by evil, but overcome evil with good.*

~ Romans 12:21 ~

Children of God should not allow the negative things in their lives to get the upper hand. They should put on the armor of God and resist the devil every day. They should be careful to do the things that God asks of them.

This can only be achieved if you know your Bible well. The guidelines that God lays down in His Word should clearly be seen in your life.

*God reveals Himself to us through His Word.*
*And we will need to give account to Him*
*for what we have done with His Word.*

~ Johan Spies ~

How do you treat your Bible?

# AUGUST

# See the image of God in people

*So God created man in his own image, in the image of God he created him; male and female he created them.*

~ GENESIS 1:27 ~

I am always amazed when I think that God, who is so holy and almighty, created people in His image and with His characteristics in them, and that He appointed us to be His ambassadors on earth.

Because you were created in God's image, you should also strive to see the image of God in others you meet, no matter how sinful or unworthy they may seem. You should live each day in such a way that you represent your Lord in a worthy manner.

*We can only be the light in this world if You renew us through Your Holy Spirit.*

~ JÖRG ZINK ~

Always remember that you are God's ambassador on earth.

# Sincere humility

*But by the grace of God I am what I am,*
*and his grace to me was not without effect.*

~ 1 Corinthians 15:10 ~

Talented people run the risk of becoming so chuffed with themselves and their achievements that they lose sight of who gave them their gifts in the first place. Not one of us has anything that we did not receive from God. Therefore we have no reason to become puffed up about anything.

Sincere humility means that you give God the glory and honor for each one of your achievements. You are what you are by the grace of God.

*Everything in this world that is beautiful and*
*good is evidence of the work of God's Spirit.*

~ Johan Cilliers ~

Do you give God the glory for
everything you achieve in life?

# Children of God

*I have been crucified with Christ and I no longer live, but Christ lives in me.*

~ GALATIANS 2:20 ~

In the letter to the Galatians, Paul writes that he has been crucified with Christ and now lives for God. His old, sinful self belongs in the past, and he no longer lives. It is Christ who lives in him.

Children of God need to be prepared to write their own obituary so that God can live in them. This is what it means to be made holy: that you decrease, and God increases.

*Holiness and love go hand in hand. If you grow in one, you will grow in the other.*

Write an epitaph for yourself in this space.

# Your own thoughts

*As water reflects a face, so a man's heart reflects the man.*

~ PROVERBS 27:19 ~

Just as a person looks in a mirror to get an idea of what he looks like, he discovers exactly who he is when he analyzes his thoughts. The things that you think are reflected in the way you live your life. If you think negative thoughts, you will be a negative person. But if you can discipline yourself to think positive thoughts, your whole life will reflect this positive approach.

You are what you think. What do you see in the mirror of your own thoughts?

*If you think you can or if you think you can't, you're right.*

~ HENRY FORD ~

What do you see reflected in the mirror of your thoughts?

# You know a person by his words

*"The good man brings good things out of the good stored up in his heart, and the evil man brings evil things out of the evil stored up in his heart. For out of the overflow of his heart his mouth speaks."*

~ Luke 6:45 ~

Out of the fullness of your heart, your mouth speaks forth. The things that reside in your heart and mind come out in the things that you say and in the way that you live. Out of the innermost parts of good people, good things come forth. But bad things will eventually come out of bad people. If you listen carefully to what people say, you will begin to understand what their hearts look like.

A tree is known by its fruit, and a person by his words.

*If your foot slips, you may recover your balance, but if your tongue slips, you cannot recall your words.*

~ Martin Vanbee ~

What do other people hear when they hear you speak?

# A mirror of God's glory

*And we, who with unveiled faces all reflect the Lord's glory, are being transformed into his likeness with ever-increasing glory, which comes from the Lord, who is the Spirit.*

~ 2 CORINTHIANS 3:18 ~

All people are born sinful. But when they are born again, their lives change completely. They become mirrors in which others can see how great and glorious is the God whom we worship.

Each Christian should reflect the glory of God. When people look at you they should be aware of God's glory. And the longer you know Him the more you should be changed into the image of Jesus.

*Whoever claims to live in him must walk as Jesus did.*

~ 1 JOHN 2:6 ~

How closely do you resemble Jesus?

# You belong to God

*There is no fear in love. But perfect love drives out fear, because fear has to do with punishment. The one who fears is not made perfect in love.*

~ 1 JOHN 4:18 ~

True love has a way of dissipating fear, as mist dissolves in the sun. Those who truly love no longer fear punishment. If there are still numerous fears in your life, it means only one thing: you are not yet completely saturated by the love of God.

Ask God to give you His love without measure. Because you belong to God, His perfect love will cause every fear in your life to flee.

*We have nothing to fear except fear itself.*
~ F. D. ROOSEVELT ~

If you are afraid, then spend more time thinking about God's love for you.

# God is not satisfied with second best

*"Yet I hold this against you: You have forsaken your first love."*

~ REVELATION 2:4 ~

In many marriages, the first passion of honeymoon love disappears after a while, and the same happens to many of us in our relationship with God. One day we wake up to find the bubbling joy that we experienced when we were born again has disappeared, and we don't love God with the fiery passion we had at first.

God is never satisfied with second best. He wants your love for Him to increase in fervor. He wants it to always be a "honeymoon" love.

*To love God requires much more than simply knowing Him.*

~ THOMAS AQUINAS ~

How much do you love God?

# Obedience to God's law

*But if anyone obeys his word, God's love is truly made complete in him. This is how we know we are in him.*

~ 1 John 2:5 ~

The love of God blossoms in those people who are obedient to the things that He asks of us in His Word. In such people, the love of God achieves its full purpose. Through our obedience to God's law and commandments we show other people that we live close to Him.

Your love for God and your obedience to His law cannot be separated from each other. The one is the natural result of the other.

*The law is never opposed to love,*
*but love is revealed through the law.*

~ Johan Heyns ~

Do you obey the Law of God?

# All-sufficient grace

*"My grace is sufficient for you, for my power is made perfect in weakness."*

~ 2 Corinthians 12:9 ~

Paul begged God to remove the thorn in his flesh, but God did not answer his prayer in the way that he wanted it answered. God told him that His grace is sufficient for him, that His strength comes to its fullest power when our strength comes to an end.

God offers you His all-sufficient grace, especially when you are at your weakest. When you have no strength, He puts His godly strength at your disposal.

*Grace is the power to face reality, to admit that sometimes things do not work out as you think they should, and yet to know that everything in your life is essentially right.*

~ Lewis B. Smedes ~

Make a list of the thorns in your flesh.

# Adversity

*Rejoice in the Lord always. I will say it again: Rejoice!*

~ Philippians 4:4 ~

The letter to the Philippians encourages us to be joyful. But this joy is specifically described: we should rejoice at all times – even when things happen that are not to our liking, even when we go through trials and tribulations because these things bring us closer to God.

To rejoice when we face adversity is difficult but it is exactly in such times that others can see that you belong to God.

*Night brings out stars as sorrow shows us truths.*

~ Philip Bailey ~

Write out Psalm 34:6 in the space below.

# Share your faith

*Consequently, faith comes from hearing the message, and the message is heard through the word of Christ.*

~ Romans 10:17 ~

God needs witnesses in His kingdom – people who will make the sharing of the gospel of Jesus Christ their life's purpose; people who will carry the good news of the salvation of Christ to those who have never heard it. No one can believe unless they have heard the gospel message.

If you believe in God, you have a responsibility not only to live out your faith, but also to share it with people around you.

*Christianity: know it in your head, stow it in your heart; show it in your life.*

~ Anonymous ~

How will you share your faith with people around you?

# The light of God

*You, O Lord, keep my lamp burning;*
*my God turns my darkness into light.*

~ Psalm 18:28 ~

The children of God can do anything when they know that God is with them. The God whom we worship makes their lamps burn brightly. His presence brings light into their lives when everything around them is dark.

If you believe in God you can courageously face all the challenges that face you. When God's light shines in your life, you will not shirk from any situation, because God is your helper. He will always turn your darkness into light.

*The sun shines on each of us alike: if you do not see it, it is because you have turned your back on it.*

Where has God turned your darkness into light?

# A heavy burden

*"Come to me, all you who are weary and burdened, and I will give you rest. For my yoke is easy and my burden is light."*

~ Matthew 11:28, 30 ~

Jesus came to offer weary, overburdened people His rest. He invites them to lay the heavy burden of their problems on His shoulders, and promises that He will give a lighter yoke in exchange.

Most of us are bone weary from carrying the burden of tomorrow's what-ifs together with the guilt of yesterday. God offers to carry your burden for you and to give you rest. Don't put off replying to His invitation.

*Nothing lasts forever, not even the difficulties you are facing.*

~ Arnold H. Glasgow ~

Are you burdened? Express your thoughts and emotions here.

# Lessons of life

*In this you greatly rejoice, though now for a little while you may have had to suffer grief in all kinds of trials. These have come so that your faith – of greater worth than gold, which perishes even though refined by fire – may be proved genuine.*

~ 1 PETER 1:6-7 ~

We all experience problems from time to time. When things in our lives test our faith, we should realize that it is actually a good thing. Just as gold is purified through fire, problems purify our lives because they test the genuineness of our faith. That is why we should rejoice when we face trials. God uses difficulties to test us at times – He wants to see if we have learned the lessons He has taught us well enough to pass them on to others.

*Each day of your life is a working day – a day on which to work on becoming the fully mature person you desire to be.*

~ JOHAN SMIT ~

How have you done in God's school of life?

# Withstand temptation

*No temptation has seized you except what is common to man. And God is faithful; he will not let you be tempted beyond what you can bear. But when you are tempted, he will also provide a way out so that you can stand up under it.*

~ 1 Corinthians 10:13 ~

God promises that He will not allow any temptation to come our way that we will not be able to resist. He promises that when temptations come our way, He will give us the strength to make the right decisions and the strength to carry through on the decisions we make.

God does not always remove the temptations in your life, but He gives you a way of escape. He shows you how you can resist those temptations.

*If God sends a difficult situation into your life,*
*He will also show you the way through it.*

What temptations do you find the most difficult to resist?

# Through all eternity

*"Will the Lord reject forever? Will he never show his favor again? Has his unfailing love vanished forever? Has his promise failed for all time? Has God forgotten to be merciful? Has he in anger withheld his compassion?" Selah*

~ Psalm 77:7-9 ~

The psalmist is heart-broken because he feels that God has abandoned him. He feels that he will never again stand within the light of God's mercy. He cannot understand why God seems to be acting so differently from the ways He has acted in the past.

If you call out to God and it seems that He does not answer you, you might be inclined to think that He has changed. But that cannot happen: God is the same yesterday, today and forever.

*God's children have one comfort: God, in whom they trust, never changes.*

God is the same day by day. He is always there for you.

# The problems of today

*Praise be to the Lord, to God our Savior, who daily bears our burdens.*

~ Psalm 68:19 ~

Many Christians become very discouraged when crises erupt in their lives. They feel as though they cannot take one more step. But it is not necessary for them to feel this way. God is ready to carry His children when times are hard. He is there to help, but He does so one day at a time.

You do not need to try to solve all the problems of yesterday and tomorrow along with all the troubles of today. Live one day at a time and you will find that you are able to handle every situation with God's help.

*We are called to carry our crosses, not drag them.*
*We should see them as a treasure, not a burden.*

~ Fénelon ~

What problems do you want to
lay at the foot of the cross today?

# Disappointments

*" Shall we accept good from God, and not trouble?"*

~ Job 2:10 ~

Even though Job experienced unbelievable hardship and pain, he still believed in God. If we accept the good things that God sends our way, then it is only logical that we should accept the bad things that come our way too, Job explains to his wife. Each person who has ever lived goes through good and bad times. Learn to accept both from God.

We are all disappointed by things that happen in our lives but we can learn through these disappointments. And remember: your disappointments are often God's appointments.

*Problems are golden opportunities.*

~ Unknown ~

What has been your greatest disappointment in life?

# Opportunities for worship

*But I will sing of your strength, in the morning I will sing of your love; for you are my fortress, my refuge in times of trouble.*

~ Psalm 59:16 ~

David wrote this psalm when he was fleeing from the soldiers Saul had sent after him to kill him. His situation left much to be desired. He prayed for God's protection and yet still found reasons to praise God in the midst of his danger. He was able to turn his crisis into an opportunity to worship God.

When you turn your crises into opportunities for worship, God will intervene in your situation and you will be able to end with a song of praise.

*Adversity is the diamond dust heaven polishes its jewels with.*

~ Robert Leighton ~

How can you turn your crisis into a golden opportunity?

# God is with you

*O Lord, the God who saves me, day and night I cry out before you. May my prayer come before you; turn your ear to my cry.*

~ Psalm 88:1-2 ~

Psalm 88 is another psalm in which the writer faced great distress. Each day he asked God to help him because his strength was gone. Things were going so badly for him that he was not far from death's door. He begged God to change his circumstances.

When you go through hard times, you can unreservedly seek help from God. The Bible assures us that God is with us during hard times. He is always prepared to help us when we ask Him.

*Those who pray do more for the world than those who go to war. If the world gets worse, it is because there are more soldiers than prayers.*

~ George Patton ~

Do you fight or do you pray?

# Trust the Lord

*I wait for the Lord, my soul waits, and in his word I put my hope.*

~ Psalm 130:5 ~

The psalmist reconfirms his trust in the Lord when he faces severe difficulties. The psalmist keeps his promise to call on other people to believe in God. God loves His children and forgives them again and again.

When the Lord allows troubles to come your way and they prevent you from serving Him wholeheartedly, He wants you to trust Him for a solution rather than just complaining.

*Commit your way to the Lord;*
*trust in Him and He will do this.*

~ Psalm 37:5 ~

Read Psalm 37.

# *God is always there for you*

*I have set the Lord always before me. Because he is at my right hand, I will not be shaken.*

~ Psalm 16:8 ~

Children of the Lord are assured that they are never alone. God is with them even when things do not go well. Because He is in their lives He ensures that they will not stumble and He keeps them safe.

When you go through difficult times, you can also be assured that God is with you. How you work through your difficulties is up to you, but the mere fact that God is always with you makes it easier from the start.

*Because God turned His back on His Son in the hour of His greatest need, you can live in His presence forever.*

You can never be without God!

# You belong to God

*When he heard this, Jesus said, "This sickness will not end in death. No, it is for God's glory so that God's Son may be glorified through it."*

~ John 11:4 ~

Sometimes things happen to God's children that we cannot understand or explain. They fall ill or lose their jobs. They pray but it seems that God does not answer. In such times they cannot understand why God does not intervene to prevent these things from happening. But God often uses disasters to bring glory to His name. He uses them to reveal His strength.

If you keep your joy and faith, and trust God when you face sickness and death, people will see that you have faith in God.

*Count each affliction, whether light or grave, God's messenger sent down to thee.*

~ Aubrey Thomas de Vere ~

Have you learned precious life-lessons through illness?

# God's comfort

*When anxiety was great within me, your consolation brought joy to my soul.*

~ Psalm 94:19 ~

The psalmist testifies that God's comfort makes him calm and peaceful in times of unrest. We all desperately need God's comfort and peace in the restless world we live in.

Pray that God will make His comfort available to you and will calm your restlessness. God's comfort can turn your restless, anxious heart into one filled with peace. He will give you an inner peace and serenity that no one will ever be able to take away from you.

*When I face heartache, I appreciate sincere sympathy. Although it cannot compensate for my loss, it does remind me that love has not died.*

~ A. C. Benson ~

If you are in need of comfort, then comfort someone else.

# Bring your anxieties to God

*"Therefore I tell you, do not worry about your life ... Is not life more important than food, and the body more important than clothes? For the pagans run after all these things, and your heavenly Father knows that you need them."*

~ MATTHEW 6:25, 32 ~

Because we belong to God we do not need to worry about the future. In the Sermon on the Mount Jesus promised us that God, who cares for the flowers and the birds, will do the same for His children.

God promises to care for you too. So you need no longer be anxious about anything. Worry gets you nowhere. Rather bring your worries to God. You will find that they will dissipate like mist before the sun.

*The fact that your anxieties monopolize so much of your attention is not because of the extent of the dangers, but because of the extent of your lack of faith.*

~ LUTHER IN A LETTER TO MELANCTHON ~

What do you do with your worries?

# Time is precious

*Be very careful, then, how you live – not as unwise but as wise, making the most of every opportunity, because the days are evil.*

~ EPHESIANS 5:15-16 ~

Each person is allocated exactly the same amount of time – twenty-four hours a day. And yet there are many people who achieve nothing with the time allotted to them while others move mountains in the same amount of time.

What do you do with the time that God has given you? Time is precious, use it effectively: you can choose to waste your time or use it profitably. You have exactly enough time each day to do just what needs to be done. Make sure that you put your time to the best use each day.

*Do not get caught up in the distant future. Take hold of the present moment. It belongs to you.*

~ SCHILLER ~

How can you make better use of your time?

# Stay quiet

*A man who lacks judgment derides his neighbor,*
*but a man of understanding holds his tongue.*
~ PROVERBS 11:12 ~

The things that we say about other people can have a big impact on their lives. And what we say about others says a lot about who we are. Someone who speaks derisively of others has little compassion. Someone who understands people will remain silent rather than drawing attention to negative things.

Do you enjoy gossiping about other people? If you have nothing positive to say about others, you should rather keep quiet.

*When thou prayest, rather let thy heart be*
*without words than thy words without heart.*
~ JOHN BUNYAN ~

If you have nothing good to say,
then rather say nothing at all.

# Praise God

*When I consider your heavens, the work of your fingers, the moon and the stars, which you have set in place, what is man that you are mindful of him, the son of man that you care for him?*

~ Psalm 8:3-4 ~

As the psalmist gazes at the wonder of God's creation, he cannot help but be impressed by the greatness and power of God. At the same time he realizes how small and insignificant he himself is. He is overwhelmed when he considers that God actually thinks about each person and cares for us.

You should take time to note the beauties of nature around each day and grow in awareness of the greatness and awesomeness of God. And you should praise Him and thank Him for the wonders of His creation.

*I cannot imagine how anyone can look up at the stars and believe that there is no God.*

~ Abraham Lincoln ~

What would you like to praise God for today?

# *Our faith is strengthened*

*Blessed are those who dwell in your house; they are ever praising you. Blessed are those whose strength is in you, who have set their hearts on pilgrimage.*

~ PSALM 84:4-5 ~

People who frequent the house of God find that things go well for them. They do not cease to praise God because they live in His presence and among other believers. These people find their strength in God.

Church attendance and fellowship with other believers is necessary because it strengthens your faith. Ensure that you do not neglect attending church services. Make sure that you feel at home in God's house.

*Without God: not a single step.*
*With God: to the ends of the earth.*

~ LIVINGSTONE ~

Do you make your home in God's home?

# God is your shepherd

*The Lord is my shepherd, I shall not be in want. Even though I walk through the valley of the shadow of death, I will fear no evil, for you are with me; your rod and your staff, they comfort me.*

~ PSALM 23:1, 4 ~

Shepherds in Bible times were expected to look after their sheep. They protected the flocks against dangers and ensured that they had sufficient food and water. And when they had to go through dangerous places, the presence of the shepherd guaranteed their safety.

If the Lord is your shepherd, He promises that His goodness and love, His strength and protection will follow you all the days of your life. You can confidently entrust your life into His hands.

*He tends his flock like a shepherd: He gathers the lambs in his arms and carries them close to his heart.*

~ ISAIAH 40:11 ~

Can you honestly say that all your needs are met?

# SEPTEMBER

# God's unconditional love

*Give thanks to the Lord, for he is good. His love endures forever.*

~ Psalm 136:1 ~

Various psalms declare the endlessness of God's love. *"His love endures forever"* is not only the introduction to Psalm 136; it appears no less than 26 times in the psalm itself.

God's unconditional love for us is the foundation of our love for one another, and the Bible assures us that there is no end to His wonderful love. Like the psalmist, we should thank and praise the Lord each day for His eternal love.

*When we invite God into our hearts, He fills our hearts with His love, because He is love. And love changes everything.*

~ Yolanda Dreyer ~

What does it mean for you personally when you remember how much God loves you?

# The promises of Jesus

*Then Jesus told him, "Because you have seen me, you have believed; blessed are those who have not seen and yet have believed."*

~ JOHN 20:29 ~

Thomas would not believe that Jesus had really risen from the dead. He insisted that he would only believe if he saw Jesus with his own eyes. When Jesus did appear to him he bowed before Him and declared his faith. But Jesus told him that people who believe without seeing are more blessed.

Ask God to increase your faith so that the phrase "seeing is believing" will no longer be part of your vocabulary. Then, without having to see, you will believe that each one of Jesus' promises is true.

*When I believe in God, I know that everything will go well for me, even when things seem all wrong.*

~ LEWIS B. SMEDES ~

Do you believe that God's promises apply to your life?

# Keep believing

*Then Jesus answered, "Woman, you have great faith! Your request is granted." And her daughter was healed from that very hour.*

~ Matthew 15:28 ~

A Canaanite woman brought her sick child to Jesus so that He could heal her. She refused to just give up when Jesus said He would not. She persisted in asking for help until finally Jesus, because of her faith, healed her child. Sometimes we ask God for things and we don't seem to get Yes for an answer. If you are prepared to keep believing and keep asking, God will fulfill your desires as long as they are in line with His will.

*The best lesson I have learned in God's school*
*is to let Him make decisions on my behalf.*
~ Dwight Moody ~

What is more important to you: your will or God's?

# Jesus can comfort you

*May our Lord Jesus Christ himself and God our Father, who loved us and by his grace gave us eternal encouragement and good hope, encourage your hearts.*

~ 2 THESSALONIANS 2:16-17 ~

Paul, in his letter, tells the Thessalonians that Jesus loves them very much. As proof of this love He comforts the Christians with the good news that they are on their way to a wonderful eternity in heaven.

When you are feeling downhearted, Jesus can comfort you because He was human just as you are. The comfort He gives you is lasting comfort that can never be taken away from you. You too can know that a wonderful future awaits you in heaven.

*The Lord does not comfort us simply so that we will be comforted, but to make us comforters.*

~ DR. JOWETT ~

Write down your favorite "comfort" Scripture verse.

# God's law

*Therefore no one will be declared righteous in his sight by observing the law; rather, through the law we become conscious of sin.*

~ ROMANS 3:20 ~

People are not set free from their sins because they keep God's law. The only thing the law can do is to show us what is right and wrong; it cannot help us not to commit sins.

God's law is a map that shows God's children how to live. Only the map of God's law can show you how to safely negotiate the land-mined terrain of sinfulness.

*The law detects, grace alone conquers sin.*

~ AUGUSTINE ~

Summarize your thoughts on law and grace.

# Talk less

*Set a guard over my mouth, O Lord; keep watch over the door of my lips.*

~ PSALM 141:3 ~

The psalmist prays that God will help him not to say the things he shouldn't. He asks that God will help him to choose his words carefully. James tells us that the person who does not stumble over what he says is perfect. He can then control the rest of his body (see Jas. 3:2).

We each have two ears and only one mouth. It would therefore seem logical that we should talk much less and become much better listeners!

*The first blow that falls in a fight is often one simple word.*
~ PHIL BOSMANS ~

Make a decision to listen more than you talk today.

# Get out of the mud bath of sin

*Do you not know that your body is a temple of the Holy Spirit, who is in you, whom you have received from God? You are not your own; you were bought at a price. Therefore honor God with your body.*

~ 1 CORINTHIANS 6:19-20 ~

Jesus paid in full for our sins with His blood on the cross. Now we need to live as people who have been set free. Our bodies are the temple of the Holy Spirit and we should glorify God with our bodies.

If you believe in Jesus, then your body is also a temple. It is impossible for Christians to wallow in the mud bath of sin and to think that they will remain clean. Live in such a way that God will be glorified in your body.

*No sin is small. No grain of sand is small in the mechanism of a watch.*

~ JEREMY TAYLOR ~

Is there one sin in your life that seems almost impossible to get rid of?

# Live out your faith

*Therefore, my brothers, be all the more eager to make your calling and election sure. For if you do these things, you will never fall.*

~ 2 PETER 1:10 ~

Peter tells us that we should grab every opportunity to live for the Lord. Through the things that we do, other people should be able to see that God called us and chose us to be His children. If we get this right then we will not continue to struggle with sins in our lives.

Does your lifestyle reflect that you belong to God? If you are prepared to live out your faith in hard times, your life will be an advertisement of your faith.

*You know that if you sin you will regret it, and yet you still do it. And that's the mystery of sin.*

~ JACO THOM ~

How will you live out your faith?

# Genuineness of faith

*In this you greatly rejoice, though now for a little while you may have had to suffer grief in all kinds of trials. These have come so that your faith – of greater worth than gold, which perishes even though refined by fire – may be proved genuine.*

~ 1 PETER 1:6-7 ~

Children of God can rejoice when they face hard times because they know that God uses these situations to bring about positive things in their lives and to determine the genuineness of their faith.

Just as the purity of gold is tested by fire, God tests the genuineness of your faith through allowing difficult situations to come your way while you are on earth. See if you can manage to rejoice when you face trials and tribulations!

*When we place everything in the hands of the sovereign and almighty God, we can face all our problems with a smile, because we know we will triumph over all our disappointments.*

~ RALPH HEINEN ~

Are you able to rejoice when you face trials?

# God's support is assured

*God has surely listened and heard my voice in prayer. Praise be to God, who has not rejected my prayer or withheld his love from me!*

~ PSALM 66:19-20 ~

The psalmist testifies that God hears his prayer and delivers him in his need. He promises that he will tell others in the congregation of how God delivered him and praise God before everyone.

We can always find help and support from God. His support is so certain that you, like the psalmist, can know that your prayer has already been heard even while you are still praying. And don't forget to honor God before your congregation when He helps you!

*Prayer is not a crutch that helps me to stand; it is the very legs on which I stand.*

~ JOHAN SMIT ~

Write down some of the times that God has helped you.

# A celebration of life

*All the days of the oppressed are wretched,*
*but the cheerful heart has a continual feast.*

~ PROVERBS 15:15 ~

If you tend to get depressed and are worried about all kinds of things, then it is pretty certain that life will not be very pleasant for you. But if you try to be cheerful each day and focus on the positive things in your life, and if you help others to focus on those things too, then your life will be a celebration.

If you make an effort to be joyful and friendly every day, your life will become a celebration and you will make the world a pleasant place for the people around you.

*Joy is the distinguishing feature of our relationship with God. The love of Christ fills our hearts with joy, always.*

~ CULES HAMMAN ~

How can you ensure that your
life is a life of celebration?

# God knows everything

*O Lord, you have searched me and you know me. You know when I sit and when I rise; you perceive my thoughts from afar.*

~ PSALM 139:1-2 ~

It is easy to hide things from people. But God knows everything. He already knows what you are thinking even before you have formulated your thoughts or put them into words. Your whole life is an open book before Him. He sees right through you. He knows all there is to know about you.

You can never hide from God. God knows everything about you. He knows each one of your hidden sins. He even knows what you think. Live so that you need never be ashamed before God.

*Sin entwines itself in our inmost being. It is the opposite of everything that is good; it is the antithesis of love.*

~ JOHAN CILLIERS ~

What little sins do you try to keep hidden?

# Tell the Lord your problems

*My soul is weary with sorrow; strengthen me according to your word.*
~ PSALM 119:28 ~

David was often worried because of the dozens of things that went wrong in his life. He often had to flee from his enemies and frequently found himself in life-threatening situations. But David knew where he could turn for help. In this psalm he testifies that God has always helped him.

If there are situations in your life that make you anxious, problems for which you cannot find solutions, tell them to the Lord – He will give you the strength to solve them.

*The only way to truly overcome anxiety is to lay it at the feet of One who never was anxious in spite of the heavy burden He carried.*
~ RALPH HEINEN ~

What causes you the most anxiety?

# God protects His children

*The Sovereign Lord is my strength; he makes my feet like the feet of a deer, he enables me to go on the heights.*

~ HABAKKUK 3:19 ~

A deer jumps from rock to rock with agility and confidence. And God protects His children and enables them to find a path through their difficulties. He wants to give you the strength you need each day and to protect you when you are in perilous situations.

Next time you face a dangerous situation in your life and it feels as if you are about to lose your footing, cling to God and, with the psalmist, declare, *"When I said, 'My foot is slipping,' your love, O Lord, supported me"* (Ps. 94:18).

*The Lord will keep you from all harm – he will watch over your life.*

~ PSALM 121:7 ~

Have you ever survived a truly dangerous situation?

# Difficulties can be beneficial

*Praise be to the God and Father of our Lord Jesus Christ, the Father of compassion and the God of all comfort, who comforts us in all our troubles, so that we can comfort those in any trouble with the comfort we ourselves have received from God.*

~ 2 Corinthians 1:3-4 ~

God promises to help His children through every difficult situation they face. But He asks that we would, in turn, do the same for other people. He wants us to help and comfort others when they go through crises. We should share the same comfort with them that we receive from God.

Difficulties can be beneficial for you. Not only do they teach you that God is always near to comfort you, but they also give you insight and sympathy for the problems that others face.

*Worry is like a rocking chair. It will give you something to do, but it won't get you anywhere.*

~ Unknown ~

Reflect on the benefits of suffering in your own life.

# Caring love

*"By this all men will know that you are my disciples, if you love one another."*

~ JOHN 13:35 ~

Just as a uniform can show what school or organization a person belongs to, our caring love for each other shows people that we belong to Christ. It is our love for other people that distinguishes us as children of God.

The way that Christians love each other is their distinctive feature. It is the one thing through which other people can see that they are different. Does your love show your friends that you belong to Jesus?

*They are the true disciples of Christ, not who know most, but who love most.*

~ FREDERICH SPANHEIM ~

How do you show others that you truly love them?

# An illustration of God's love

*"A new command I give you: Love one another.*
*As I have loved you, so you must love one another."*

~ JOHN 13:34 ~

When Jesus was on earth, He exemplified the love of God each day. He was always prepared to help other people. He healed the sick, gave the lame the ability to walk, the deaf the ability to hear and the blind their sight. Jesus really cared for other people, and this was illustrated in His actions.

Just as Jesus was a living illustration of the love of God on earth, He wants us to be examples of His love to others.

*We must learn to love without hidden*
*agendas or in exchange for gifts and favors.*
~ JAN DU RAND ~

How can you become a living example of God's love?

# Be thankful always

*Give thanks in all circumstances, for this is God's will for you in Christ Jesus.*

~ 1 THESSALONIANS 5:18 ~

To be constantly thankful is a way of life. It means that you no longer take things for granted but will remember that everything we have is a gift of God's undeserved grace. Paul, in his letter to the Thessalonian Christians, wrote that it is not enough simply to be thankful; they should be thankful in every situation.

Through faith you can succeed in being thankful in all circumstances. It is often in these difficult situations that God hones you to be a better witness for Him.

*Happy people are not those who have the most, but those who are the most grateful for what they have.*

~ W. J. OEHLER ~

Try to thank God for something new every day.

# God's perfect love

*Do not be anxious about anything, but in everything, by prayer and petition, with thanksgiving, present your requests to God. And the peace of God, which transcends all understanding, will guard your hearts and your minds in Christ Jesus.*

~ Philippians 4:6-7 ~

Children of God have no need to worry about anything. All they need to do is tell God about the things they really want, and at the same time to thank Him because He will give them what they ask for. People who get this right live with the peace of God in their lives.

Praise and thanksgiving go hand-in-hand. Once you discover this, you can give the many fears in your life to God in exchange for His perfect peace.

*We can reject God's love, but we can do nothing that will convince Him to stop loving us.*

~ Ampie Barnard ~

Write out your favorite Bible verse about God's love.

# Our broken world

*Blessed is he whose help is the God of Jacob, whose hope is in the Lord his God.*

~ PSALM 146:5 ~

Things always go well for the people who depend on God and who go to Him for help. They know that they can confidently keep trusting in God because, in spite of the fact that they live in a broken world, He is preparing a new world for their future.

Our broken world fits into God's Master Plan. Because He is always in control, you can always put your hope in Him. You have Jesus' promise that He has gone to prepare a place for you in heaven.

*When you say a situation or person is hopeless, you are slamming the door in the face of God.*

~ CHARLES ALLEN ~

Write out your favorite Bible verse about hope.

# God will support you

*The Lord upholds all those who fall and lifts up all who are bowed down.*
~ Psalm 145:14 ~

The psalmist knows that God is always there for people who are tired and discouraged. He supports those who are oppressed. That is why even though many of the psalms begin on a negative note, by the end of the psalm the writers are much more positive. Things are not necessarily better for them but they have faith that God will support them as He has done in the past.

When you feel depressed and discouraged, God promises that He will hold you up and support you. Trust Him to do so!

*Those who walk through the deep darkness*
*of depression develop an inner strength that*
*makes them wiser than they were before.*
~ Marietjie van Rooyen ~

Write down some of the occasions where
God has supported you in the darkness.

# God knows you personally

*What is man that you are mindful of him,*
*the son of man that you care for him?*
~ PSALM 8:4 ~

God is great and almighty while people are insignificant and transitory. There are millions and millions of people in the world, and yet God knows each one of His children. He knows us personally.

God who is so great and almighty knows you personally, too. He knows your name, He thinks about you, He came to offer His love to you – the Bible assures us of all this. And anyone who touches you, touches the apple of His eye!

*I have summoned you by name; you are mine.*
~ ISAIAH 43:1 ~

Isn't it wonderful to know that
God cares so much about you that even
the hairs on your head have been counted?

# Trust in the Lord

*When I called, you answered me; you made me bold and stouthearted. The Lord will fulfill his purpose for me; your love, O Lord, endures forever – do not abandon the works of your hands.*

~ PSALM 138:3, 8 ~

The children of God never call on Him in vain. He always stands ready to help them succeed and He is always prepared to offer His miracle working power to them. That is why, in the long run, things always turn out well for those who trust in Him.

If you trust in the Lord you will be capable of doing great things because He promises you His help, support and strength.

*It takes courage, faith, self-discipline and trust to hand the reins of your life to God. It requires wisdom and insight to be able to look beyond earthly, human limitations.*

~ YOLANDA DREYER ~

Can you think of an example when God caused things to work out well for you?

# The love of God

*This is how we know who the children of God are and who the children of the devil are: Anyone who does not do what is right is not a child of God; nor is anyone who does not love his brother.*

~ 1 JOHN 3:10 ~

There are different ways that our love for the Lord can be proved: those people who do not do what is right, or those who do not love their fellowman are definitely not children of the Lord. Their father is the devil.

By loving all those around you with the love of God, you make Him visible to the world. This is the guarantee that you belong to Him. Ask God to give you an abundance of His love so that it will overflow and touch all those people you come into contact with.

*Let no debt remain outstanding, except the continuing debt to love one another, for he who loves his fellowman has fulfilled the law.*
~ ROMANS 13:8 ~

How do you make the love of God visible to others?

# On the right road

*Whoever loves his brother lives in the light,*
*and there is nothing in him to make him stumble.*

~ 1 John 2:10 ~

It is possible to differentiate between people who live in the light of God's presence from those who wander around in the darkness of sin by looking at the way they treat other people. Those who love their fellowman live in the light and God Himself will show them the right road through life. Those who do not love others remain in darkness.

If you love others with the love with which God loves you, this love will keep you on the right road and keep you from stumbling.

*God's love has an eternal influence on us.*
~ Yolanda Dreyer ~

How do you live when no one is watching?

# Little faith

*But when he asks, he must believe and not doubt, because he who doubts is like a wave of the sea, blown and tossed by the wind. That man should not think he will receive anything from the Lord.*

~ JAMES 1:6-7 ~

When you pray but do not receive what you pray for, you should carefully consider whether your unanswered prayers are perhaps the result of your lack of faith. Do you really believe that God can – and will – give you what you ask for? If you still doubt, you should not expect to receive anything from the Lord.

The reason that you have so many unanswered prayers is because you have such little faith. People who doubt do not receive much of what they ask God for in prayer.

*When you think of faith, you should also immediately think of obedience and patience.*

~ FRANCOIS THERON ~

Do you believe that God will answer your prayers?

# A child of God

*If anyone considers himself religious and yet does not keep a tight rein on his tongue, he deceives himself and his religion is worthless.*

~ James 1:26 ~

Many people say that they are Christians but if you listen to their conversations, you find it hard to believe your ears! They gossip about others, pass on all kinds of untruths and half-truths, and sometimes use swear words and even take the Lord's name in vain. James warns that people who think that they are spiritual but who cannot control their tongues, deceive themselves.

Be warned! If you are a child of God your conversation should show it, otherwise your religion is worthless.

*We can measure the love we have for our fellowman with the words of our tongues.*

~ Maretha Maartens ~

Is your conversation sprinkled with kind and uplifting words?

# Depend on God

*But even if I am being poured out like a drink offering on the sacrifice and service coming from your faith, I am glad and rejoice with all of you.*

~ PHILIPPIANS 2:17 ~

The faith of the Philippians is a sacrifice in the service of God, says Paul. Even if his blood should be poured out as a drink offering to the Lord, he would still rejoice. His death would help the Philippians to serve God even better.

Faith is not always easy because it requires you to recognize your own limitations and to confess your dependence on God. Only when you realize that you can do nothing on your own, will you develop the kind of faith that God longs for His children to have.

*Faith means standing back so that*
*God can stand up on your behalf.*

~ JOHAN SMIT ~

What has your faith cost you?

# In difficult situations

*When I said, "My foot is slipping," your love, O Lord, supported me.*

~ Psalm 94:18 ~

Things happen to each one of us that threaten to knock us off our faith of feet. Then we even begin to question God's love for us. When circumstances threaten to knock you off your feet, God puts His faithful love at your disposal. Hold fast to that and you will stay standing.

You can lean on God when you go through hard times. His faithful love is always there to support you when you cannot stand on your own.

*Only when you are ready to admit your own inability*
*and know, without a shadow of a doubt, that only*
*God can help you, can you begin to talk of faith.*

~ Johan Smit ~

What things have caused your faith to grow stronger?

# Keep each of your promises

*When you make a vow to God, do not delay in fulfilling it. He has no pleasure in fools; fulfill your vow. It is better not to vow than to make a vow and not fulfill it.*

~ ECCLESIASTES 5:4-5 ~

We tend to make vows and promises to God very glibly when we are in tight spots. But when things begin to get better we often forget the promises we made. The preacher in Ecclesiastes says that we should not let this happen. What we promise to do must be followed through. If you do not think you can keep your promises, you should rather not make any.

Keep every promise you make – to people as well as to God. It is better not to promise anything than to be unfaithful to your promises.

*The highest kind of faith is when you build your hope for life, your hope for the future, on the promises of God alone.*

~ I. L. DE VILLIERS ~

Do you keep your promises to God and others?

# OCTOBER

# Everything comes from God

*For who makes you different from anyone else?*
*What do you have that you did not receive?*

~ 1 Corinthians 4:7 ~

We are all innately selfish. Secretly we like to think that we're just a little better than the next person. In our eyes there is no one quite as important as us! This is particularly true if we have been successful and other people look up to us. But the truth is that not one of us has anything that we did not receive from God. It is easy to become swollen-headed when we do very well. But remember that you have nothing that did not come from God.

*Every day I tell God: You are wonderful. The more I say this, the more my eyes are opened to His great wonders.*

~ Phil Bosmans ~

Do you give God the glory for the successes in your life?

# God's love is unconditional

*You are my God, and I will give you thanks;*
*you are my God, and I will exalt you. Give thanks to*
*the Lord, for he is good; his love endures forever.*

~ Psalm 118:28-29 ~

The Bible has much to say about the extent of God's love. *"The earth is full of his unfailing love ... Your love, O Lord, reaches to the heavens, your faithfulness to the skies,"* writes the psalmist (Ps. 33:5 and 36:5). And above all, His love is unconditional.

God's love for you is unending and unrestricted. It does not depend on your good points. It continues forever – in spite of your faults and weaknesses.

*God loved us before the foundations of the world so that we, together with His only begotten Son, could be His children.*

~ Augustine ~

Try to write a definition of God's love.

# God is your Father

*For you did not receive a spirit that makes you a slave again to fear, but you received the Spirit of sonship. And by him we cry, "Abba, Father."*

~ Romans 8:15 ~

The word Abba is the intimate term a child would use when he talks to his dad. It is only through the Holy Spirit that we are able to call the great Creator Dad. He makes us children of God and ensures that an unbreakable bond forms between the Father and us.

The presence of the Holy Spirit in your life is your personal spiritual birth certificate. Because He lives in you, you can now call God your Father.

*The Holy Spirit is the initial deposit of the fullness of our redemption.*

~ Willie Jonker ~

Write a spiritual birth certificate for yourself.

# God shows His love

*May our Lord Jesus Christ himself and God our Father, who loved us and by his grace gave us eternal encouragement and good hope, encourage your hearts.*

~ 2 THESSALONIANS 2:16-17 ~

If we ever doubt the extent of God's love for us, we simply need to look at Jesus on the cross. God loves us so much that He sent His only Son to be crucified so that, if we believe in Him, we will live forever. This is the meaning of grace. It is the indisputable evidence of God's love.

If you persist in the faith God will demonstrate His love, grace, comfort, and hope in your life.

*The way God loves is unchanging and beyond understanding.*

~ AUGUSTINE ~

In what ways can you see God's love for you in your life?

# The discipline of God

*The Lord disciplines those he loves, and he punishes everyone he accepts as a son.*

~ Hebrews 12:6 ~

When the Lord loves someone, He shows him what He expects of him, even though it might sometimes be painful. He acts like parents who truly love their children, and so chastise them because they love them. They want to keep their children on the right road.

No one likes going through painful experiences, but remember that more often than not God's discipline is proof of His love for you – people don't punish children who are not their own!

*It takes both rain and sunshine to make a rainbow.*

~ Unknown ~

Do you think discipline is really necessary?

# Share in His glory

*God disciplines us for our good, that we may share in his holiness.*

~ Hebrews 12:10 ~

It is never pleasant to be punished, but it is good for us. Children who are chastised, later reap the positive fruits of the punishment that has been issued. Someone who learns his lesson through being punished becomes a person who is obedient to God. Such a person is fully committed to God.

God's discipline is always for your best. He draws you closer to Himself through it. And then you will be able to share in His glory.

*We grow in holiness as we grow in love.*

~ Ralph Martin ~

What lessons have you learned from being chastised?

# Peace and prosperity

*Submit to God and be at peace with him;*
*in this way prosperity will come to you.*
~ JOB 22:21 ~

When Job rebelled against God because he could not understand why he was being so unfairly punished, his friend Eliphas encouraged him to allow God to teach him through what he was experiencing. When your relationship with God is right and you willingly submit yourself to Him, you will live in peace and God will cause you to prosper.

It is only when you are prepared to yield completely to God that you will have peace and prosperity in your life.

*The peace that the world gives, is the peace of escape. The peace that Jesus wants to give, is the peace of victory.*
~ WILLIAM BARCLAY ~

What effect has God's peace had in your life?

# People's problems

*If you spend yourselves in behalf of the hungry and satisfy the needs of the oppressed, then your light will rise in the darkness, and your night will become like the noonday ... Then you will call, and the Lord will answer; you will cry for help, and he will say: Here am I.*

~ Isaiah 58:10, 9 ~

God expects His children to be finely tuned when other people go through hard times and to support them in their trials. If we are prepared to help others, then God promises to help us when we call to Him in our distress. He will always be available to provide for us when we go through hard times.

If you see others in distress and help them, God will hear and answer your prayers and will be with you when you really need Him.

*A person who claims not to need anyone and will not give to others what they need, lives a lonely life.*

~ Dagobert Runes ~

Are you a caring person?

# You need never be afraid

*Then he got up and rebuked the winds and the waves, and it was completely calm.*

~ Matthew 8:26 ~

The disciples were surprised when Jesus stilled the storm at sea with only a few words. They could not understand how the wind and the waves obeyed Him.

Not only does God have power over nature, but He also has power in the lives of His children. That is why you can confidently ask Him to help you when storms rise up in your life. Jesus is able to still every storm in your life. That is why, with Him, you need never again be afraid.

*He who fears man does not fear God; he who fears God, no longer fears man.*

~ Dietrich Bonhoeffer ~

Are you able to exchange your fear for faith?

# God holds you close

*The eternal God is your refuge, and underneath are the everlasting arms.*

~ Deuteronomy 33:27 ~

God is a hiding place for His children, a hiding place from all dangers. And He promises that His arms are always beneath His children to hold them up.

When life knocks you off your feet, you can confidently trust in God. He promises to keep you safe. And even more – in such times you can know that God is holding you securely. He is your hiding place and His eternal arms are always beneath you.

*The great burden we all carry is the weight of our sin about the past combined with the weight of our sinful anxiety about tomorrow.*

~ Johan Smit ~

Do you have a safe refuge in times of danger?

# Hard times

*Praise be to the Lord, to God our Savior, who daily bears our burdens.*

~ PSALM 68:19 ~

The journey of a thousand miles begins with a single step, says the well-known proverb. A long journey consists of many single steps. And in the same way it is easier to handle hard times one day at a time.

God promises to carry you day by day, not year by year or month by month. Trust Him daily to help you in your hard times and learn to live one day at a time.

*We can trust because to trust is to realize that*
*God has won the victory over the calamities of life.*

~ JOHAN HEYNS ~

Rate your level of trust in God on a scale of 1-10.

# You are strong in Him

*"My grace is sufficient for you, for my power is made perfect in weakness."*

~ 2 Corinthians 12:9 ~

If we believe that we are strong enough to handle the problems in our lives on our own, we will quickly discover how wrong we are. But if we depend on God's strength then things are very different. As soon as we acknowledge our own lack of strength, God puts His strength at our disposal.

When you are strong enough to identify your weaknesses, God's strength will be fully deployed in your life. When you are weak, then you are strong in Him.

*I think it is good advice not to worry too much about tomorrow and the day thereafter. We should rather avail ourselves of God's offer of strength for each day as it comes.*

~ Johan Smit ~

God wants to make His strength available to you today.

# God promises to help us

*"'If you can'?" said Jesus. "Everything is possible for him who believes." Immediately the boy's father exclaimed, "I do believe; help me overcome my unbelief!"*

~ Mark 9:23-24 ~

There was no one who could heal the desperate father's disabled son. That is why they struggled to believe that Jesus could do it. But Jesus told him that everything is possible for those who believe. The father confessed his faith on the grounds of this statement and asked Jesus to help him in the areas where he still struggled to believe.

It is completely possible to believe in God and yet still to harbor doubts. In such times of doubt, God promises to help you overcome your unbelief.

*Faith is the only light we have on the future.*
~ Theodore Hoecker ~

Have you ever believed, and
yet doubted at the same time?

October 14

# Do not be discouraged

*Say to those with fearful hearts, "Be strong, do not fear; your God will come, he will come with vengeance; with divine retribution he will come to save you."*

~ Isaiah 35:4 ~

There is no one who has the same amount of courage day after day. Sometimes our situation is so hopeless that even with the best will in the world we cannot seem to keep hoping in God.

Does it feel as though you are near breaking point today? If you know God, you need never be discouraged. He can deliver you out of every difficulty and can give you new strength and courage each day. Therefore, be strong, do not be afraid. Your God is here!

*Be strong and courageous.*

~ Deuteronomy 31:6 ~

List the things that want to make you give up, but remember that you have a God who is greater than your problems.

# Pray about your concerns

*Do not be anxious about anything, but in everything, by prayer and petition, with thanksgiving, present your requests to God. And the peace of God, which transcends all understanding, will guard your hearts and your minds in Christ Jesus.*

~ PHILIPPIANS 4:6-7 ~

Often we find ourselves filled with anxiety kneeling next to our beds to talk to God. But when we trust Him with our desires and anxieties, He gives us peace in our hearts and minds. Then we leave the place of prayer in peace.

When we face severe challenges, God offers us His peace that passes all understanding. If you would like to experience God's peace, you must learn to pray about all your concerns.

*When you learn to bring your problems to God,*
*He will care for you in every detail of your life.*

Write down your worries in a prayer to God.

# The peace of God

*Peace I leave with you; my peace I give you. I do not give to you as the world gives. Do not let your hearts be troubled and do not be afraid.*

~ John 14:27 ~

When Jesus bade farewell to His disciples, He told them that He was going to His Father. And at the same time He promised that He would leave His peace with them. The peace that He gives is different from the peace the world gives. People who have the peace of Jesus in their lives have no need to worry or fear.

Not only does Jesus bring you peace with God, but also the peace of God. You can make His peace part of your life today.

*The Lord blesses his people with peace.*
~ Psalm 29:11 ~

What things take away your peace?

# Keep hoping

*Against all hope, Abraham in hope believed and so became the father of many nations, just as it had been said to him, "So shall your offspring be."*

~ ROMANS 4:18 ~

Abraham knew that it was no longer possible for God's promise of descendents through him to be fulfilled. Neither he nor his wife could have children. But still he refused to give up hope. He continued to believe that God's promise would come to pass, no matter what happened.

If, like Abraham, you can continue to hope, even when it seems that all grounds for hope are past, then, like him, you will reap the fruit of faith in God's perfect timing.

*Hope is born when we rise above our own despair and become involved in the joy and pain of those around us.*

~ JÜRGEN MOLTMANN ~

Write down the reasons that you continue to hope.

# Renewed relationships

*Therefore, since we have been justified through faith, we have peace with God through our Lord Jesus Christ.*

~ Romans 5:1 ~

We see little of the kind of peace the Bible describes in our own lives. All around us we see unrest and violence. But God can still give His children peace. Because we believe in Him, He sets us free to live in peace with Him and with other people.

Peace on earth can best be described as a ceasefire. God's peace refers to renewed relationships: with Him, with ourselves, and with others.

*All men desire peace, but very few desire those things that make for peace.*

~ Thomas à Kempis ~

What can you do to live at peace with others?

# Peace in your heart and life

*I will listen to what God the Lord will say; he promises peace to his people, his saints – but let them not return to folly.*

~ Psalm 85:8 ~

The psalmist writes that the Word of God brings peace to His people, to those who faithfully serve Him. If you make God's Word part of your life, then it will bring about peace in your life. Through His Word, you hear Him speak personally to you each day.

Listen carefully to everything that God says to you. If you are obedient to Him, you will experience His peace in your heart and life.

*The Bible offers us the foundational constitution for dealing with life and the problems it presents.*

~ Willie Jonker ~

Why do you think our country needs peace first and foremost?

# Lasting peace

*For he himself is our peace.*
~ Ephesians 2:14 ~

Peace is not actually a common noun, but a Person, Paul explains to the Ephesians: Christ is our peace. Because He came into the world it is possible for peace to exist between God and mankind, and between people themselves.

Make sure that you are never without this peace. The peace that Jesus gives is lasting. Because it comes from within, nothing that ever happens to you can take that peace away.

*Peace is not something that we dream about. It is something that we make, that we do. It is part of who we are and is something that we can give to others.*
~ Robert Fulghum ~

Has Jesus become your peace?

# Be prepared to be used by God

*Therefore, my dear friends, continue to work out your salvation with fear and trembling, for it is God who works in you to will and to act according to his good purpose.*

~ PHILIPPIANS 2:12-13 ~

It is not all that hard to live as children of God and to do the things He asks us to do. In the long run, God simply wants us to be prepared to be used by Him. If we are willing, He will equip us and help us to do His will.

God will equip you and enable you to do the things that He expects of you. All that you need to do is to be prepared to be used by Him.

*To walk in God's will, we must listen to the voice of His Holy Spirit. If something we want to do is in God's Will, He will give us peace in our heart, and our uncertainty will dissipate.*

~ ARNOLD MOL ~

What do you think is God's will for your life?

# You have today

*This is the day the Lord has made; let us rejoice and be glad in it.*

~ Psalm 118:24 ~

Each new day that God gives to His children is a reason to rejoice. It is a day that we can enjoy fully and in which we can do the things we really want to do.

Not one of us knows how many days are left of our lives here on earth. You cannot know how many tomorrows lie ahead of you. But you do have today. Use each moment fully today and enjoy the day. Don't put off for tomorrow what you can do today.

*If you want to do something, do it now. Apologize if you need to, show how much you love someone. Where there has been discord, make peace. Don't waste time.*

~ Daphne Fairley ~

Do what needs to be done today.

# Hard times strengthen your faith

*We also rejoice in our sufferings, because we know that suffering produces perseverance; perseverance, character; and character, hope.*

~ ROMANS 5:3-4 ~

Christians can really rejoice when they go through hard times because they have discovered a special secret: hard times form and fashion them so that their faith in God increases. It also helps them to develop a strong Christian character and to believe. Through thick and thin they believe that God's new world waits for them.

Rejoice in your trials and tribulations. Difficulties are always a catalyst that strengthen your faith and give you a brighter hope in God.

*Faith is the daring of the soul to go further than it can see.*

~ WILLIAM NEWTON CLARKE ~

How have past difficulties increased your faith?

# Share your heartache with God

*Hear my prayer, O Lord, listen to my cry for help;*
*be not deaf to my weeping. For I dwell with you*
*as an alien, a stranger, as all my fathers were.*

~ Psalm 39:12 ~

The psalmist begs God to listen to his prayer, to hear his cry for help, and not to be unmoved by his tears. He is convinced that the Lord will protect him and that He will care for him in his times of despair.

When sorrow comes your way, the best advice you can follow is to share your pain with God. He is always ready to comfort you, to help you and to care for you.

*I have never met with a single instance of adversity which I have not in the end seen was for my good – I have never heard of a Christian on his deathbed complaining of his afflictions.*

~ Alexander Proudfit ~

What is your greatest sorrow in life?

# The beauty of nature

*"Listen to this, Job; stop and consider God's wonders. Do you know how God controls the clouds and makes his lightning flash? Do you know how the clouds hang poised, those wonders of him who is perfect in knowledge?"*

~ JOB 37:14-16 ~

God made this world wonderfully well – and He knows all things. When he took Job for a walk through the beauties of His creation, Job realized for the first time how great His wonders are. Finally he knew that God owed him nothing and that people have no right to question God.

Don't ever walk blindly through the wonders and beauties of nature, and don't forget to bow in adoration before the Creator of all things.

*The world is charged with the grandeur of God.*
*it will flame out, like shining from shook foil.*

~ GERARD MANLY HOPKINS ~

What three things do you find the most beautiful?

# Spread the knowledge of Him

*For we are to God the aroma of Christ among those who are being saved and those who are perishing.*

~ 2 CORINTHIANS 2:15 ~

God can do all things, but on earth He chooses to work through His children. He needs us to spread the knowledge of Jesus among the people around us. He uses us wherever we are to make other people aware of Jesus.

God wants your life to be a testimony that rises like incense before Him. He wants to spread the knowledge of Himself through you so that everyone in the world will get to hear His good news first hand.

*God wants to spread the aroma of the knowledge of Him through your life.*

How are you going to share the good news of the gospel with others?

# Reach out

*And over all these virtues put on love, which binds them all together in perfect unity. Let the peace of Christ rule in your hearts, since as members of one body you were called to peace. And be thankful.*

~ Colossians 3:14-15 ~

The most important commandment that God asks of His children is that they love each other. This love is the bond that binds Christians together in perfect unity. And people who love each other in this supernatural way also have God's peace.

When Christians decide to be united and to reach out to one another in love it will automatically lead to mutual peace.

*Love makes us sensitive to the needs of others.*

~ Jan van der Watt ~

Are you able to love all people?

# Do not prescribe to God

*"Father, if you are willing, take this cup from me; yet not my will, but yours be done."*

~ LUKE 22:42 ~

Sometimes we ask God for things in such a way that we insist on getting our own way. But that's not how prayer works. In Gethsemane Jesus earnestly prayed that God would remove the cup of suffering from Him, but He was still prepared to subject His will to God's will.

Make very sure that you don't prescribe to God when you come to Him in faith. And don't be disappointed and upset if God answers your prayers differently from how you would have liked the answers to come.

*The value of persistent prayer is not that God will eventually hear us, but that we will eventually hear Him.*

~ WILLIAM MCGILL ~

Are you prepared to drink the cup of suffering in your life?

# The secret of contentment

*Better what the eye sees than the roving of the appetite.*
~ Ecclesiastes 6:9 ~

Very few people are satisfied with what they have. We always want more money, a better car, a smarter house and so we forget to be thankful for all those things that God has already given us. What we have is better than what we long for, says the writer of Ecclesiastes.

Therefore, be satisfied with what you have. When you discover that the things you already have are better than the things you think you want, you will have found the secret to contentment.

*Anxieties and concerns drive us to prayer, and prayer drives away anxieties and concerns.*
~ Melancthon ~

What will bring you contentment and satisfaction?

# Experience His presence

*He makes me lie down in green pastures, he leads me beside quiet waters.*

~ PSALM 23:2 ~

Psalm 23 presents us with a pastoral picture of peace and rest: of green hills and peaceful waters and a shepherd who watches over his sheep and who ensures their peace and safety.

God wants to be your shepherd. In a world of unrest and violence He wants to create a living space for you where you can be happy and safe, and where you will experience His peace and His presence every day.

*Father, fill my restless heart with peace. The world cannot give us peace. Let us, therefore, experience the truth of Your promise that nothing can take away the peace You give us.*

~ KIERKEGAARD ~

How does knowing that God is your shepherd affect your life?

# God's comfort

*"Blessed are those who mourn, for they will be comforted."*
~ MATTHEW 5:4 ~

All those who mourn over the pain and hardship of this world are blessed because God Himself will wipe away their tears and comfort them, so Jesus taught in the Sermon on the Mount. The Bible promises us that all our heartache will come to an end when Jesus returns.

You are actually blessed and happy when you sorrow and mourn. People whose hearts are aching have a need for God's comfort and your pain gives you the sensitivity to comfort others in their pain.

*The soul would have no rainbow had the eye no tears.*
~ JOHN VANCE CHEYNEY ~

How can you comfort someone whose heart is broken?

# NOVEMBER

# God offers you eternity

*For our light and momentary troubles are achieving for us an eternal glory that far outweighs them all.*

~ 2 Corinthians 4:17 ~

Our difficulties in this world cannot be compared to the wonderful things that await us in God's new world. And what's more, our times of suffering last for only a short time. God's children will eventually experience a glory that far surpasses our greatest expectations. And it will last for ever.

All earthly problems are merely temporary. Anchor your hope in God who offers you eternal life.

*The final test of faith is when you can sing in the darkest night.*

~ Johan Smit ~

Read the description of the new Jerusalem in Revelation 21.

# Message of hope

*Always be prepared to give an answer to everyone who asks you to give the reason for the hope that you have.*

~ 1 PETER 3:15 ~

When people ask us about the things that God has promised to His children, and which we anticipate so eagerly, we should always be ready to give them an answer and to tell them about our hope. This is the advice Peter gives us.

You too need to be prepared to talk to others about the hope that lives in you. Each Christian carries God's hope – and the responsibility of conveying this message of hope to others rests on you.

*To continue to hope when you cannot see is to walk along the road God has shown you and not to be by dead end streets, or to let walls prevent you from going further. It is to persevere as one who sees the invisible God.*

~ JOHAN CILLIERS ~

Do you reflect God's hope?

# God has always been your help

*The Lord is my strength and my shield; my heart trusts in him, and I am helped. My heart leaps for joy and I will give thanks to him in song.*

~ PSALM 28:7 ~

When the psalmist begins to feel discouraged because things are going so wrong in his life, he reminds himself that God has always helped him the past. That is why he can gladly believe that God will do so again in the future.

Faith always relies on specific knowledge. You know that God will help you because He has always been your help. Trust Him, and praise Him!

*We can continue to trust, because trusting God means that we acknowledge that God has overcome the dangers of life.*

~ JOHAN HEYNS ~

When you begin to despair remember how God helped you in the past.

# *Your life will change*

*If you confess with your mouth, "Jesus is Lord," and believe in your heart that God raised him from the dead, you will be saved.*

~ ROMANS 10:9 ~

In his letter to the Romans, Paul explains that it is very easy to be saved. All that you need to do is to confess with your words that Jesus Christ is Lord and believe in your heart that God raised Him from the dead.

Faith and testimony always go hand in hand. And faith and testimony are required of every child of God. If you believe in God and bear witness to Him then your whole life will change.

*I reckon him a Christian indeed who is not ashamed of the Gospel, nor a shame to it.*

~ MATTHEW HENRY ~

Do you believe, and do you testify of God's goodness?

# *God offers you His mercy*

*Yet the Lord longs to be gracious to you;*
*he rises to show you compassion. For the Lord is a*
*God of justice. Blessed are all who wait for him!*

~ ISAIAH 30:18 ~

The prophet Isaiah had a message for the people: God was waiting for an opportunity to show them the extent of His great mercy toward them. He was ready to intervene in their negative circumstances at any moment because of His compassion for them.

And God is waiting to be merciful to you too. He never treats you as you deserve. He offers you His grace and mercy and eagerly waits for you to accept it.

*As grace is first from God, so it is continually*
*from him, as much as light is all day long from*
*the sun, as well as at the first dawn or at sun-rising.*

~ JONATHAN EDWARDS ~

God will pour His grace into each of your negative situations, if you but ask Him to.

# Heavenly glory

*Christ in you, the hope of glory.*

~ COLOSSIANS 1:27 ~

Christ lives in each of His children through His Holy Spirit. He made it possible for us to go to heaven one day where we will live with Him forever. He makes it possible for us to hold fast to the hope of the heavenly glory that awaits us.

The Christian's whole life is determined by the fact that he hopes in Christ. He earned heavenly glory for each one of His children on the cross.

*Remember that hope is actually*
*a person: the Lord Jesus Christ.*

In what do you place your hope?

# Reconciled with God

*"Blessed are the peacemakers, for they will be called sons of God."*

~ MATTHEW 5:9 ~

Blessed are those people who not only have the peace of God in their lives but who also commit themselves to be peacemakers between people, said Jesus. These peacemakers will be called the children of God.

Before you can become a peacemaker you first need to have the peace of Jesus in your own life, and that is only possible if you have been reconciled to God through Christ. When that happens you will begin to promote peace between people.

*Reconciliation is needed where relationships have been broken.*

Dedicate yourself to being a peacemaker.

# Acknowledge your own weaknesses

*"Who is like you, O Lord? You rescue the poor from those too strong for them, the poor and needy from those who rob them. Vindicate me in your righteousness, O Lord my God; do not let them gloat over me."*

~ PSALM 35:10, 24 ~

God has a soft spot for people who are willing to admit their own weaknesses. He sets them free from enemies that are much stronger than them. The psalmist asks that God will do this for him, and that He will always act fairly toward him.

God will set you free from people who are stronger than you are. But sometimes God first wants you to acknowledge your weaknesses before He will reveal His strength to you, and cause justice to triumph.

*The greatest burden we have to carry in life is self; the most difficult thing we have to manage is self.*

~ HANNAH WHITALL SMITH ~

Write your weaknesses and faults in the space below.

# Don't give up

*Praise be to the Lord, to God our Savior, who daily bears our burdens.*

~ Psalm 68:19 ~

God's children can justly praise Him because He supports them each day. He carries them when they cannot take another step, and helps them when they need assistance.

When you feel as though you cannot go on, don't give up. Try to live each day to the full and trust God for tomorrow. And remember to praise Him every day for His help and faithfulness.

*When you come to the end of your strength,*
*you are only at the beginning of God's.*

Don't give up!

# God holds you tight

*In my integrity you uphold me and set me in your presence forever.*

~ PSALM 41:12 ~

A crying baby is soothed very quickly when his mother picks him up and holds him in her arms. In her arms, he feels safe and secure. The same is true for the children of God. It is reassuring to know that God holds us tight and close to His breast at all times. We are always safe with Him.

God holds His children by the hand. He holds you tight. He is always close to you. He makes sure that you stay near to Him. And in that truth, you can find fullness of peace.

*I would rather walk with God in*
*the dark than go alone in the light.*

~ MARY BRAINARD ~

You are always safe when you are close to God.

# Eternal life

*"I give them eternal life, and they shall never perish; no one can snatch them out of my hand."*

~ JOHN 10:28 ~

Jesus told His disciples that He would give eternal life to all those who believe in Him. They will never, through all eternity, be lost because no one can pluck them out of His hand. One day they will be with Him in heaven forever.

This promise is meant for you too. If you believe in Jesus, then heaven is yours. He guarantees you eternal life and no one will ever take you out of His hand.

*Life is not payment for services rendered, but a gift of grace. And there is only one thing to do with a gift: enjoy it!*

~ JOHAN HEYNS ~

Do you know for certain that you will live forever?

# Pray without ceasing

*"And will not God bring about justice for his chosen ones, who cry out to him day and night? Will he keep putting them off? I tell you, he will see that they get justice, and quickly. However, when the Son of Man comes, will he find faith on the earth?"*

~ Luke 18:7-8 ~

Jesus promises that God will listen to His children if they call out to Him day and night. He will not let them wait long for an answer. He will bring them an answer, and quickly at that! All that they need to do is to keep praying.

Sometimes you might get discouraged when you keep on praying and don't receive an answer from God. God promises in His Word that He will help you, and it will be quick. Just keep up your courage for a little while longer!

*He who stops praying, stops growing.*
~ W. G. Benham ~

Pray continually! (1 Thes. 5:17)

# In the arms of God

*"As a mother comforts her child, so will I comfort you; and you will be comforted over Jerusalem."*

~ Isaiah 66:13 ~

There is only one place where a baby feels completely safe – in his mother's arms. Just as a mother makes her baby feel safe, so God promises to ensure the safety and security of His people.

In the arms of God you will find help and security, stability and safety. With His arms around you, you have nothing to fear. With Him you are safe forever.

*The eternal God is your refuge, and underneath are the everlasting arms.*

~ Deuteronomy 33:27 ~

God holds you in His arms, always.

# *God is mighty*

*"You are worthy, our Lord and God, to receive glory and honor and power, for you created all things, and by your will they were created and have their being."*

~ Revelation 4:11 ~

Only God is worthy to receive glory and honor and power because He created all things. This is the testimony of the twenty-four elders when they prostrate themselves before the throne of God in worship. He alone is the Creator of everything and everyone. It was through His will that the world and all in it came into existence.

God is great, wonderful, almighty, and glorious. He is the Creator of all things. Always remember to praise God, to thank Him and give Him the glory that is due to His name.

*Dare to dream. We serve a God*
*who delights to do the impossible.*
~ Andrew Murray ~

What do you enjoy most in God's creation?

# Serenity

*Finally, brothers, whatever is true, whatever is noble, whatever is right, whatever is pure, whatever is lovely, whatever is admirable – if anything is excellent or praiseworthy – think about such things. Whatever you have learned or received or heard from me, or seen in me – put it into practice. And the God of peace will be with you.*

~ PHILIPPIANS 4:8-9 ~

Stress and anxiety first make their appearance in your thoughts. Therefore, if you can learn to focus your thoughts on the right things then God, who guarantees peace in your life, will give you His peace.

Try to think only restful, relaxing thoughts and suppress the fearful thoughts that try to surface. What you think about will determine whether you become a tense, harried person or whether you will have serenity and peace.

*Our thoughts are important, because as we think, so we are.*
~ RALPH HEINEN ~

Focus your thoughts on the things of God.

# Obedience to God

*No discipline seems pleasant at the time, but painful. Later on, however, it produces a harvest of righteousness and peace for those who have been trained by it.*

~ Hebrews 12:11 ~

When a naughty child is disciplined, he realizes that his punishment was for his benefit. Through being punished he learns not to do the things that are wrong. Later on he discovers that the discipline he received was actually good for him because it taught him to be obedient. *"Before I was afflicted I went astray, but now I obey your word"* (Ps. 119:67). Enduring difficulties almost always produces the fruit of peace in your life, because through them you learn to be obedient to God.

*In the way of righteousness there is life; along that path is immortality.*
~ Proverbs 12:28 ~

How obedient are you to God?

# Renewed day by day

*Therefore we do not lose heart. Though outwardly we are wasting away, yet inwardly we are being renewed day by day.*

~ 2 CORINTHIANS 4:16 ~

Christians need never be discouraged. Even in the most difficult times they can persevere because God is always with them. Each day He renews them from within.

Christians have a light that not even the darkest night can extinguish. It does not matter how bad things are on the outside, God renews you day by day within your heart. And to top it all, you have the assurance that God will be with you whenever you go through hard times.

*Courage is not the absence of fear.*
*Courage is facing fear and overcoming it*
~ R. L. STEVENSON ~

Write down why you need never give up hope.

# *God listens to your prayers*

*O people of Zion, who live in Jerusalem, you will weep no more. How gracious he will be when you cry for help! As soon as he hears, he will answer you.*

~ ISAIAH 30:19 ~

Isaiah comforts the grieving people of God. He tells them that they can wipe away their tears. God promises to be merciful to them if they call on Him. He will answer their prayers as soon as He hears them.

This word of comfort is meant for you too. Sometimes it feels as though God is deaf to your pleas when you call out to Him. But that is not possible. He is a merciful God who hears and answers each one of your prayers.

*Prayer is the golden key that opens heaven.*
~ THOMAS WATSON ~

Write down the request that you would like to bring to God today.

# God's greatness

*But God made the earth by his power; he founded the world by his wisdom and stretched out the heavens by his understanding. When he thunders, the waters in the heavens roar; he makes clouds rise from the ends of the earth.*

~ Jeremiah 10:12 ~

In this passage Jeremiah describes the greatness of God. It was God who, through His might, brought the world into existence. When we consider His awesome works in creation, and hear His voice through all His works, we begin to realize how foolish we are and how little we know. It is only when you meditate on the greatness of God that you begin to realize your own insignificance and sinfulness. Make time to worship this awesome God.

*Praise is like a plow that makes deep furrows*
*in the heart of a believer so that God's glory*
*can come forth in every aspect of our lives.*
~ C. M. Hanson ~

Praise God for His greatness.
Write your own psalm to honor Him.

# True love

*Dear children, let us not love with words or tongue but with actions and in truth. And this is his command: to believe in the name of his Son, Jesus Christ, and to love one another as he commanded us.*

~ 1 JOHN 3:18, 23 ~

When Jesus was asked to identify the most important commandment in the Word of God, He did not hesitate to state that it is to love God above all else, and to love others as we love ourselves. God commands His children to love one another. This is not a debatable issue. And this love needs to be seen in our actions. True love is never just a theory. It is always practical. Your love for the Lord is seen in what you do.

*Love is more easily defined than it is demonstrated.*
~ UNKNOWN ~

Is your love evident in what you do?

# God's love for you

*"For God so loved the world that he gave his one and only Son, that whoever believes in him shall not perish but have eternal life."*

~ JOHN 3:16 ~

God loved the world so much that He chose to give His Son so that all those who believe in Him will not be lost but will live forever. God's love is a giving love. It is a love that asks nothing in return.

God's love never asks what it will get from you but always seeks to see what it can give. And this is the kind of love you should foster for other people.

*To love is to see a glimpse of heaven.*

~ KAREN SUNDE ~

Ask God to fill your heart with His compassion.

# Broken at the cross

*"I tell you the truth, he who believes has everlasting life. I am the bread of life."*

~ JOHN 6:47-48 ~

Jesus called Himself the bread of life. And He explained that all those who believe in Him already have eternal life. But His body had to be broken on the cross to make eternal life possible for you and me. The cost of turning sinners into children of God was very high.

Faith brings life. Just as we break the bread in communion, Jesus' body was broken for you on the cross so that everyone who believes could receive life.

*The man who cannot continue to believe in God when all around him things go wrong, has not yet understood what faith is.*

~ CHARLES SPURGEON ~

Jesus died for you. What are you doing to show your gratitude?

# For your good

*And we know that in all things God works for the good of those who love him, who have been called according to his purpose.*

~ ROMANS 8:28 ~

There is one thing that Christians can be certain of: God has a purpose with everything He allows to happen in their lives. Even the negative things are used to bring about His goal. For those people who love God, those whom He has called to be His children, everything works together for good.

And God knows what's best for you too. He causes all things to work together for your good if you truly love Him.

*Doubt is part of our life with God, because we still live in a dispensation where God allows man to question Him.*

~ I. L. DE VILLIERS ~

God will cause all things to work together for your good. Believe that it is so.

# The Lord will help you

*But I trust in you, O Lord; I say, "You are my God." My times are in your hands; deliver me from my enemies and from those who pursue me. Be strong and take heart, all you who hope in the Lord.*

~ PSALM 31:14-15, 24 ~

The psalmist discovered that he could trust God at all times because his whole life was under God's control. That is why he was able to be strong in all circumstances and not give up hope.

Everything that happens to you – even the difficult things – are part of God's plan for your life. If you trust in Him, He will help you. You too can be strong and courageous, even in the midst of a severe crisis.

*Those who trust in God depend on Him alone who holds all things in His hands, who can speak one word and bring all affliction that would otherwise destroy us, to an end.*

~ SISTER BASILICA ~

No one who trusts in God is ever disappointed.

# God gives you more

*Now to him who is able to do immeasurably more than all we ask or imagine, according to his power that is at work within us, to him be glory in the church and in Christ Jesus throughout all generations, for ever and ever! Amen.*

~ Ephesians 3:20-21 ~

Sometimes the children of God receive very little from Him because they expect so little from Him. God is strong and mighty. His strength is at work in each of His children. He is willing and able to do things for us beyond our wildest dreams, and He gives us far more that we ask of Him.

The God in whom you believe is almighty. He is in a position to give you infinitely more than you ask for. His mercy goes far beyond your prayers and expectations. Always give honor to Him.

*Grace needs to be nurtured, and it is in nurturing it that we realize how precious it really is.*

~ Johan Smit ~

What would you like God to do for you?

# Nothing is impossible

*Jesus looked at them and said, "With man this is impossible, but not with God; all things are possible with God."*

~ MARK 10:27 ~

It is not appropriate to judge God by what is humanly possible. Our limitations do not apply to Him. He can make the impossible possible because He is a God of miracles. History shows that God frequently intervenes in the lives of His children in miraculous ways. He is still the same God, and is able to do the same for you today.

God can hear and answer each one of your prayer requests. He has solutions for each of your problems. Nothing is impossible for Him.

*O Lord, You are my God; I will exalt You and*
*praise Your name, for in perfect faithfulness You*
*have done marvelous things, things planned long ago.*

~ ISAIAH 25:1 ~

God is able to perform miracles in your life.

# The attributes of God

*So God created man in his own image, in the image of God he created him; male and female he created them.*

~ GENESIS 1:27 ~

When God created people, He created them in His image, with something of His nature in them. People, unlike animals, can distinguish between right and wrong, can love people and can worship God.

There is part of God's nature in you too. Your character and emotions should therefore reflect something of the nature of God. Live in such a way that people who observe you will notice a flicker of God's light in you.

*Live in such a way that wherever you go you will be able to take your place as God's ambassador.*

Reflect on what it means to have been made in the image of God.

# God notices you

*I pray also that the eyes of your heart may be enlightened in order that you may know the hope to which he has called you, the riches of his glorious inheritance in the saints, and his incomparably great power for us who believe. That power is like the working of his mighty strength, which he exerted in Christ when he raised him from the dead.*

~ Ephesians 1:18-20 ~

We cannot grasp the immensity of God's unlimited might with our human understanding. But the truly remarkable thing is that God not only puts His might, which is stronger than anything else, at our disposal, but also causes that power to work through us.

God is aware of you. He has a special plan for your life. Because you are His child, His illimitable power is at work in your life. With such power available to you, you are literally capable of anything.

*I can do everything through him who gives me strength.*
~ Philippians 4:13 ~

God knows what you are going through, and He makes His strength available for you to use.

# *Gifts of grace*

*But to each one of us grace has been given as Christ apportioned it.*

~ EPHESIANS 4:7 ~

When we begin to compare our average gifts and talents with those of much more gifted friends, we tend to become a little disgruntled and wonder why God passed us over. If this has been the case in your life, have a look at the special abilities that God has entrusted to you.

Even though we have not all been given the same gifts of grace, God has not overlooked even one of us. He has given each one of us a gift that can be used in His service. Use yours to honor Him!

*If you commit yourself to doing your very*
*best with the talents and abilities you have,*
*nothing can stop you from being successful.*
~ WILLEM CRUYWAGEN ~

What skills and abilities would you most like to have?

# Hold fast to the promises of God

*Let us hold unswervingly to the hope we profess, for he who promised is faithful.*

~ HEBREWS 10:23 ~

God's children can confidently hold fast to every promise of God that is recorded in His Word. God always does what He has promised to do. Hope is a word that focuses on the future. Therefore you can continue to hope in the promises that God will bring to pass in your life. And you can remind Him of these promises.

You can hold onto the promises of God in difficult times because He cannot be unfaithful to His promises.

*If you are tired of trying to reach the stars to bring a little light into the lives of others, go and sit quietly for a while and listen to the Creator of all things.*

~ ANONYMOUS ~

Write your favorite Bible promise in the space below.

# DECEMBER

# He died on the cross

*Since you are precious and honored in my sight, and because I love you, I will give men in exchange for you, and people in exchange for your life.*

~ ISAIAH 43:4 ~

Each person is precious in God's sight. We are so precious that He gives people in our place, nations so that we might live. And He gives even more. He was prepared to give His Son to die on the cross in our place. Jesus gave us His life in exchange for our sins.

You, too, are precious to God. He knows you by name. He knows all there is to know about you. He loves you so much that He gave His only Son to die for you on the cross.

*Jesus died so that you can live.*
*Show your gratitude by the way you live.*

When you feel as if your life is worthless,
remember how precious you are in God's eyes.

# Faith

*And without faith it is impossible to please God, because anyone who comes to him must believe that he exists and that he rewards those who earnestly seek him.*

~ Hebrews 11:6 ~

It is impossible to live as God expects us to if we do not believe in Him. If you really want to stay close to Him and make His will paramount in your life, it is imperative to believe that He exists and that He receives with open arms those people who seek Him.

Faith is the only thing that can bring you into a right relationship with God. And it is only God who can cause faith to work in your heart.

*Faith does not mean to trust without evidence, but to trust without reservations.*

~ Elton Trueblood ~

What do you understand by faith?

# God gives you light

*Who among you fears the Lord and obeys the word of his servant? Let him who walks in the dark, who has no light, trust in the name of the Lord and rely on his God.*

~ ISAIAH 50:10 ~

Dark times come into the lives of every person. In these dark times God wants to be the light in the lives of His children. He wants to offer us His help when we go through crises. We simply need to take Him at His word, and trust Him. He is always with us when times are hard. And He will cause all things to work together for our good.

God gives you light when you can see no light. He causes things to work out well even when things look dark.

*No night is so dark that it can extinguish the light of the Morning Star. This light shines the brightest when things around are at their darkest.*

God always works with your best interests at heart.

# Believe in Jesus

*For it is by grace you have been saved, through faith – and this not from yourselves, it is the gift of God.*

~ EPHESIANS 2:8 ~

There is only one way that people can be saved: by believing in Jesus. We cannot bring about our own salvation. It is a gift that comes to us from God alone. And He gives it to us because of His grace. All that we need to do is to receive His gift with thankful hearts.

You cannot satisfy God's requirements through what you do, and neither can you do anything to earn your salvation. But you can satisfy Him by believing in Jesus.

*I do not try to understand so that I can believe; I believe so that I can understand.*

~ ST. ANSELM OF CANTERBURY ~

How can you please God?

# He will make you well

*I have heard your prayer and seen your tears; I will heal you. On the third day from now you will go up to the temple of the Lord.*

~ 2 KINGS 20:5 ~

When King Hezekiah became fatally ill, he prayed that God would heal him. And God answered Hezekiah's prayer. He promised to heal him, and said that he would be able to go to the temple the very next day.

When you deal with sickness in your life you can be sure that God will hear your prayer and heal you, if that is His will. And even if you do not get well, you can bear testimony to Him from your sickbed.

*The Great Physician knows His patients so well that He will never prescribe the wrong medicine for them.*

~ MARETHA MAARTENS ~

Has God ever healed you when you were sick?

# God is aware of your heartache

*Record my lament; list my tears on your scroll – are they not in your record?*

~ PSALM 56:8 ~

The psalmist experienced times of great heartache. In these times he was comforted when he remembered that God knew about his anguish and that He saw each tear the psalmist cried. Each one was recorded in God's book. God is never unmoved when His children's hearts are breaking.

God is aware of your heartache – each tear of yours is recorded in His book! He really cares for you. And He eases the heartache of each one of His children.

*Heartache prepares us to receive joy and appreciate it more fully.*
~ JOHAN SMIT ~

What has saddened your heart today? Tell God about it.

# Wisdom and tact

*Peacemakers who sow in peace raise a harvest of righteousness.*

~ JAMES 3:18 ~

James writes that anyone who needs wisdom can confidently ask God for it. He is prepared to give His wisdom to anyone who asks Him for it (see Jas. 1:5-6). His wisdom teaches us to live differently from the way we lived before, and to enter into a right relationship with God and to live in peace with our fellowman.

To be a peacemaker in this world requires tact and wisdom – the kind of wisdom that only God can give you. Ask Him for it.

*There is no shortcut to wisdom. It does not require a special education, but experience. Through the circumstances of our lives we gain understanding and insight.*

~ PIET NAUDÉ ~

If you lack wisdom, ask God to give you His.

# In heaven

*"There will be no more death or mourning or crying or pain, for the old order of things has passed away."*

~ REVELATION 21:4 ~

When John was given a revelation of God's new world, he discovered that things in heaven will be very different from the world that we know. No one will die there. Sorrow and suffering and pain will be things of the past. The children of God will be happy with God forever.

In hard times you can think about the eternal glory that God has promised to give you. With God in heaven there will be an end to all anguish, unhappiness and pain.

*The grave is not a dead-end street. It is a passage. It ends with the sunset, and awakens with the true light of day.*

~ VICTOR HUGO ~

What do you think heaven will be like?

# God gives joy after the sorrow

*Those who sow in tears will reap with songs of joy.*
*He who goes out weeping, carrying seed to sow, will*
*return with songs of joy, carrying sheaves with him.*

~ PSALM 126:5-6 ~

God promises His children joy after sorrow. After the heartache of the exile, God's people could return to their own land with joy because God made a way for them. The people who sow in tears can, in faith, look forward to the day when they will reap the harvest in joy.

God can change your circumstances. He always turns sorrow into joy. He wants to turn your heartache into an abundant harvest today.

*It is pointless to ask God to make our lives*
*happy when we refuse to yield to Him.*

~ C. S. LEWIS ~

What can you rejoice in today?

# Talk to Him in prayer

*Train yourself to be godly.*

~ 1 TIMOTHY 4:7 ~

Christians need to practice how to serve God, just as an athlete practices to stay fit, so wrote Paul to Timothy. If we really want to live a life committed to God, it will require sacrifice and practice on our part. And this kind of practice is much more important than physical exercise because it prepares you for heaven. If you wish to be spiritually fit, you need to make time for God. Study your Bible regularly and talk to Him in prayer.

*Prayer is a conversation between*
*two people who love each other.*

~ ROSALIND RINKER ~

Are your prayers conversations,
or are they monologues?

# *He walks with you*

*For a man's ways are in full view of the Lord, and he examines all his paths.*

~ PROVERBS 5:21 ~

God knows everything there is to know about His children. Their lives are an open book before Him. He even sees each step they take.

Because God loves you, He walks with you each step of the way through life. Not only does He accompany you, but He examines each one of your steps! God knows all that you do and say and knows exactly what you need. He gives you strength to victoriously overcome each challenge that comes your way.

*God is interested in you. He knows exactly what you need moment by moment.*

What does it mean to know that God walks by your side?

# Life is a race

*Let us run with perseverance the race marked out for us. Let us fix our eyes on Jesus, the author and perfecter of our faith.*

~ Hebrews 12:1-2 ~

The children of God have a head start in the race of life. They know the secret of how to look away from the obstacles in their way and to look to God. And they also know that He will help them to the end of the course, and that they will end the race as victors if they trust in Him.

Your life here on earth is a race. Only if you keep your eyes on Jesus will you have the spiritual strength that will keep you in the race till the end.

*Great works are performed not*
*by strength but by perseverance.*
~ Samuel Johnson ~

Learn to focus on God rather than on your problems.

# God looks after His children

*Praise awaits you, O God, in Zion; to you our vows will be fulfilled. You crown the year with your bounty, and your carts overflow with abundance.*

~ PSALM 65:1, 11 ~

The psalmist sings a praise song to God as the harvest is gathered in. He remembers that it is God who sends the rain that causes the grain to grow so that the animals will have sufficient food. It is God who makes the harvest grow and crowns the year with His gifts. Wherever He goes, He gives in abundance.

Just as God cares for creation around you, He also cares for each one of His children. When your life lines up with His will then it will become a song of praise.

*Cast your cares on the Lord and he will sustain you; he will never let the righteous fall.*

~ PSALM 55:22 ~

God promises to care for you.

# God protects you

*The angel of the Lord encamps around those who fear him, and he delivers them.*

~ PSALM 34:7 ~

We read many accounts in the Old Testament of how God protected His children and rescued them from danger. When they were in distress, He was always there to help them.

God is still able to protect His children. God knows about every distressing situation in your life. In such times He erects a hedge round about you to protect you. Ask for His help when you need Him.

*For he will command his angels concerning you to guard you in all your ways.*

~ PSALM 91:11 ~

God sends His angels to look after you.

# The Holy Spirit defends you

*In the same way, the Spirit helps us in our weakness. We do not know what we ought to pray for, but the Spirit himself intercedes for us with groans that words cannot express.*

~ ROMANS 8:26 ~

God gives His Holy Spirit to each of His children to teach us the right way to communicate with Him. When we don't know how to pray, when we cannot find the right words to offer in our petitions, then the Holy Spirit presents our case for us. He carries our requests directly to the throne room of God.

Just as an advocate defends a criminal in court, when you sin, the Holy Spirit defends your position before God.

*The Holy Spirit is the initial deposit*
*of the fullness of our redemption.*

~ WILLIE JONKER ~

Ask the Holy Spirit to teach you to pray.

# Make yourself available to Him

*"I am the Lord's servant," Mary answered.*
*"May it be to me as you have said."*
~ Luke 1:38 ~

Even though the angel brought a seemingly impossible message to Mary – that she would give birth to a Son even though she was a virgin – she was immediately prepared to make herself available for God to use. She did not give a thought to the problems that she would experience. She was prepared to obey God at once.

God can turn your problems into blessings if you are prepared to make yourself available to Him. If you are willing to do this, He will undertake to solve your problems.

*Faith does not ask questions; doubt finds no answers.*
~ A. M. Wells ~

Are you prepared to make
yourself available for God to use?

# No place for Jesus

*She gave birth to her firstborn, a son. She wrapped him in cloths and placed him in a manger, because there was no room for them in the inn.*

~ LUKE 2:7 ~

Bethlehem was crowded because of the census. Joseph and Mary were not able to find place in an inn and so the Son of God was born in a dirty stable. It was there that Mary gave birth to Him, wrapped Him in swaddling cloths and made Him a crib in the animal's feeding trough.

When Jesus was born there was no room for Him in the inn. And today there are still many people who make no room for Him in their hearts and lives.

*Never get so busy that you have no time for Jesus.*

Make time for Jesus in your life.

# Good news

*When they had seen him, they spread the word concerning what had been told them about this child.*

~ LUKE 2:17 ~

The wonderful news the angels brought – that the long awaited Savior of the world had been born in Bethlehem – was joyfully received by the shepherds. After the angels departed, they left everything just as it was and hurried to Bethlehem where they found Joseph, Mary and the Baby in a stable. They told them everything the angels had said about the Child.

When they left, they told the good news of the Savior's birth to everyone they saw. Do you tell others about the Good News that you have heard?

*I tell you the truth, we speak of what we know, and we testify to what we have seen, but still you people do not accept our testimony.*

~ JOHN 3:11 ~

Are you a messenger of the good news of God?

# A child of God

*For you know the grace of our Lord Jesus Christ, that though he was rich, yet for your sakes he became poor, so that you through his poverty might become rich.*

~ 2 CORINTHIANS 8:9 ~

Jesus is so good to us – good beyond our understanding. He put aside the honor and glory that were His due for the sake of sinful people. He was prepared to come into the world as an ordinary person, to be poor, so that all those who believe in Him can inherit the riches of heaven.

Jesus, the great King of all kings, was prepared to leave heaven and to be born as a baby so that you could become a child of God.

*I believe that the greatest test of human greatness is found in true humility.*

~ JOHN RUSKIN ~

Jesus sacrificed heaven on your behalf.
What will you sacrifice for Him?

# Without fear

*But the angel said to them, "Do not be afraid. I bring you good news of great joy that will be for all the people. Today in the town of David a Savior has been born to you; he is Christ the Lord."*

~ Luke 2:10-11 ~

The shepherds were initially terrified when they first saw the angel. But the angel calmed their fears. He told them that they had nothing to fear because the message that he brought was one of great joy: the Savior who had been expected for so long had been born at last.

Christians can live without fear. You need no longer be afraid of anything because your Savior was born two thousand years ago in Bethlehem.

*When you learn not to fear you will discover how wonderful it is to remain strong in the face of suffering.*

~ Longfellow ~

What are you afraid of?

# He is with you every day

*"Fear not, for I have redeemed you; I have summoned you by name; you are mine."*

~ ISAIAH 43:1 ~

Isaiah the prophet had a message of joy for the children of God: they could confidently unpack their burdens at His feet and leave them there and walk unimpeded through life. The God whom they worshiped set them free. He called them by name. They are His, both now and forever.

And this wonderful Redeemer is with you each day too. He lives in you through His Holy Spirit, and He protects and helps you.

*The Lord said that He will come as a thief in the night, therefore we do not need to fear the night.*

~ HEINRICH JUNG-SCHILLING ~

Do not be afraid. God is with you.

# Always with you

*"The virgin will be with child and will give birth to a son, and they will call him Immanuel" – which means, "God with us."*

~ MATTHEW 1:23 ~

The prophet Isaiah declared that God would give a sign to His people: a virgin would one day give birth to a Son. And the child would be called Immanuel, which means God is with us. He was the One who would set His people free from their sins (Is. 7:14).

This prophecy came to pass on the first Christmas. Jesus was born of a virgin. And through His birth, God wants to let you know that He is always with you.

*God forsook His Son on Golgotha so that we need never live apart from Him.*

God has promised never to leave you.

# The light conquers eternally

*The true light that gives light to every man was coming into the world. The Word became flesh and made his dwelling among us. We have seen his glory, the glory of the One and Only, who came from the Father, full of grace and truth.*

~ John 1:9, 14 ~

Isaiah also prophesied that the people who lived in darkness would see a great light (see Is. 7:1). John explained that Jesus, who is the true light of God, came into this world. He is the Word of God who became flesh and lived amongst us. Jesus came to shine a light in our world darkened by sin. When He was born, the light overcame the darkness once and for all.

*Even a single candle can make*
*a difference in the darkest night.*

~ Johan Smit ~

Let your life reflect the light of God in this world.

# Jesus existed from the beginning

*That which was from the beginning, which we have heard, which we have seen with our eyes, which we have looked at and our hands have touched – this we proclaim concerning the Word of life.*

~ 1 JOHN 1:1 ~

Jesus was not just an ordinary person. He is God Himself. He has always existed. And yet ordinary people could hear Him speak, they could see Him and could even touch Him with their hands. Jesus came to make it possible for people to approach God openly. Before He came to earth, no one could see God and live.

Jesus has always existed. He is the Word and the Life. He came to earth to make a way for you to live with God forever.

*Faith is the scarlet thread interwoven in the tapestry of my life. It is the red knot that brings all the other strands together.*

~ BERTA SMIT ~

Jesus has always existed. How does this affect your life?

# The greatest gift

*Thanks be to God for his indescribable gift!*

~ 2 CORINTHIANS 9:15 ~

Jesus is the most wonderful gift of all time. Because God gave Him to the world on that first Christmas, He, through His death on the cross, made it possible for anyone who believes in Him to become children of God. We should never stop thanking God for Him.

When you and those you love give Christmas gifts to each other, you should not forget to thank God for Jesus Christ – He is the most wonderful gift that anyone could ever receive.

*We give each other gifts at Christmas to celebrate the greatest Gift that God gave when He sent Jesus into this world.*

What does Christmas mean to you?

# Peace in our land

*Because of the tender mercy of our God, by which the rising sun will come to us from heaven to shine on those living in darkness and in the shadow of death, to guide our feet into the path of peace.*

~ Luke 1:78-79 ~

The prophet Zechariah prophesied that the Child that was to be born would be like the morning sun. He would cause the grace of God to shine in all the world and bring light to the people who still lived in the shadow and darkness of death. He would make it possible for them to follow the path of peace.

Peace in our country with its great variety of people is only possible in a future where every citizen knows Jesus personally.

*Peace remains a distant dream until we have learned a greater lesson: the pain and freedom that comes from repentance and forgiveness.*

~ Buks van Tonder ~

What are you doing to promote peace in this country?

# *His goodness is yours*

*For his anger lasts only a moment, but his favor lasts a lifetime; weeping may remain for a night, but rejoicing comes in the morning.*

~ PSALM 30:5 ~

God does not stay angry for long, but His faithful love for His children lasts for ever. Jesus earned forgiveness for us when He died on the cross, and so God is no longer angry with us because of our sins. But this does not guarantee that His children will be free from difficulties.

When dark times come into your life, you can trust in God. He is always there to help you and to solve your problems for you. His anger lasts for a moment, but His goodness is with you your whole life long.

*Jesus is the suffering servant who understands our pain, who is with us and on our behalf bears its burden.*

~ JOHAN CILLIERS ~

God's love for you and His goodness last forever.

# According to God's will

*"Therefore I tell you, whatever you ask for in prayer, believe that you have received it, and it will be yours."*

~ MARK 11:24 ~

Jesus assured His disciples that when people pray and believe, they will receive what they ask of God. And yet there is a condition attached to this promise: God does not answer prayers that are not in accordance with His will.

When you pray according to God's will, you can be so sure that He will answer you that you can thank Him even before you see the answer to your prayer.

*Bring your requests to God, and then say, "Your will be done!"*

~ DWIGHT MOODY ~

Try to pray in accordance with the will of God.

# Look past the problems

*I believed; therefore I said, "I am greatly afflicted."*

~ PSALM 116:10 ~

Over and again the psalmist experienced God's deliverance when his life was in danger. In these challenging times he could still keep believing in God, even when he thought there was no way out.

Trust and faith still work in the midst of crises. Even though your troubles might sometimes seem insurmountable, you can look past them and see God. You can keep believing in Him even when you think there's no hope.

*When things look impossible, we can be assured that God can make the impossible possible.*

~ MARTIN LUTHER ~

Trust God when you face a crisis in your life.

# In the future

*But you will not leave in haste or go in flight; for the Lord will go before you, the God of Israel will be your rear guard.*

~ ISAIAH 52:12 ~

God assures His people that they do not need to flee helter-skelter from Babylon. He promises to go ahead of them to lead them and to protect them from behind.

Just as God has walked with you through the year that has passed, He wants to be with you each day of the future. He wants to walk ahead of you into the new year. He will go before you to show you the way, and He will be behind you to keep you safe.

*God promises never to leave you. He will be with you in the future, just as He was in the past.*

God holds your future in His hand.

# The right road

*Whether you turn to the right or to the left, your ears will hear a voice behind you, saying, "This is the way; walk in it."*
~ ISAIAH 30:21 ~

We all at times lose our way and take a detour from God's path. If this should happen to you, God promises that you will hear a voice behind you that will direct you on the right path.

In the year that has passed, you experienced God with you each day. And He wants to lead you into the new year. Make sure that you are sensitive to His voice.

*If the Lord delights in a man's way, he makes his steps firm.*
~ PSALM 37:23 ~

Listen carefully for the voice of God
as you follow your path through life.